HARRIS COUNTY PUBLIC LIBRARY

3 4028 05

D0772750

MAJOR
PRESIDENTIAL ELECTIONS
and the administrations that followed

The Election of
1860

and the Administration of
Abraham Lincoln

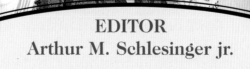

EDITOR
Arthur M. Schlesinger jr.

ASSOCIATE EDITORS
Fred L. Israel & David J. Frent

The Elections of 1789 & 1792 and the Administration of George Washington

The Election of 1800 and the Administration of Thomas Jefferson

The Election of 1828 and the Administration of Andrew Jackson

The Election of 1840 and the Harrison/Tyler Administrations

The Election of 1860 and the Administration of Abraham Lincoln

The Election of 1876 and the Administration of Rutherford B. Hayes

The Election of 1896 and the Administration of William McKinley

The Election of 1912 and the Administration of Woodrow Wilson

The Election of 1932 and the Administration of Franklin D. Roosevelt

The Election of 1948 and the Administration of Harry S. Truman

The Election of 1960 and the Administration of John F. Kennedy

The Election of 1968 and the Administration of Richard Nixon

The Election of 1976 and the Administration of Jimmy Carter

The Election of 1980 and the Administration of Ronald Reagan

The Election of 2000 and the Administration of George W. Bush

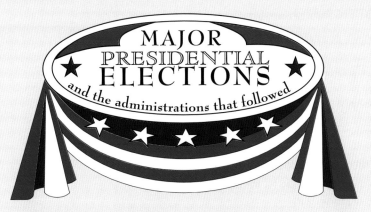

MAJOR PRESIDENTIAL ELECTIONS
and the administrations that followed

The Election of
1860

and the Administration of Abraham Lincoln

EDITOR

Arthur M. Schlesinger, jr.
Albert Schweitzer Chair in the Humanities
The City University of New York

ASSOCIATE EDITORS

Fred L. Israel
Department of History
The City College of New York

David J. Frent
The David J. and Janice L. Frent
Political Americana Collection

Mason Crest Publishers
Philadelphia

Produced by OTTN Publishing, Stockton, New Jersey

Mason Crest Publishers
370 Reed Road
Broomall PA 19008
www.masoncrest.com

Contributing Editor: Christopher Higgins
Research Consultant: Patrick K. Hilferty
Editorial Assistant: Jane Ziff

First printing

1 3 5 7 9 8 6 4 2

Library of Congress Cataloging-in-Publication Data

The election of 1860 and the administration of Abraham Lincoln / editor, Arthur M. Schlesinger,
Jr. ; associate editors, Fred L. Israel & David J. Frent.
    p. cm. — (Major presidential elections and the administrations that followed)
Summary: Provides an overview of the election of 1860 and the administration of President
Abraham Lincoln, using a variety of source materials.
    Includes bibliographical references and index.
    ISBN 1-59084-355-X
1. Presidents—United States—Election—1860—Juvenile literature. 2. Presidents—United
States—Election—1860—Sources—Juvenile literature. 3. United States—Politics and
government—1861-1865—Sources—Juvenile literature. 4. United States—Politics and
government—1861-1865—Juvenile literature. 5. Lincoln, Abraham, 1809-1865—Juvenile
literature.   [1. Presidents—Election—1860—Sources. 2. United States—Politics and
government—1861-1865—Sources. 3. Lincoln, Abraham, 1809-1865.]
I. Schlesinger, Arthur Meier, 1917-   . II. Israel, Fred L. III. Frent, David J. IV. Series.
E440.E44 2003
973.7'092—dc21

                                                      2002011261

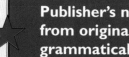

**Publisher's note: all quotations in this book come
from original sources, and contain the spelling and
grammatical inconsistencies of the original text.**

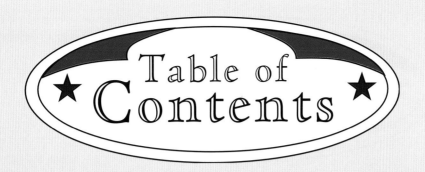

Table of Contents

Introduction 6
   Arthur M. Schlesinger jr.

The Election of 1860 17
   William E. Gienapp

Facts at a Glance..38

1858 "House Divided" Speech 43

Republican Party Platform of 1860 49

Democratic Party Platforms 55

Constitutional Union Platform 59

The Crittenden Compromise 61

Lincoln's First Inaugural Address.................................67

Message to Congress, July 4, 1861 79

The Homestead Act of 1862...89

The Pacific Railway Act..95

Letter to Horace Greeley...99

The Emancipation Proclamation 101

The Gettysburg Address..105

Lincoln's Plan for Reconstruction 107

Lincoln's Veto of the Wade-Davis Bill.........................113

The Wade-Davis Manifesto 115

Lincoln's Second Inaugural Address 119

Further Reading...122

Index 124

★ INTRODUCTION ★
Arthur M. Schlesinger, Jr.

America suffers from a sort of intermittent fever—what one may call a quintan ague. Every fourth year there come terrible shakings, passing into the hot fit of the presidential election; then follows what physicians call "the interval"; then again the fit.

—James Bryce, *The American Commonwealth* (1888)

Running for president is the central rite in the American political order. It was not always so. *Choosing* the chief magistrate had been the point of the quadrennial election from the beginning, but it took a long while for candidates to *run* for the highest office in the land; that is, to solicit, visibly and actively, the support of the voters. These volumes show through text and illustration how those aspiring to the White House have moved on from ascetic self-restraint to shameless self-merchandising. This work thereby illuminates the changing ways the American people have conceived the role of their President. I hope it will also recall to new generations some of the more picturesque and endearing dimensions of American politics.

The primary force behind the revolution in campaign attitudes and techniques was a development unforeseen by the men who framed the Constitution—the rise of the party system. Party competition was not at all their original intent. Quite the contrary: inspired at one or two removes by Lord Bolingbroke's British tract of half a century earlier, *The Idea of a Patriot King*, the Founding Fathers envisaged a Patriot President, standing above party and faction, representing the whole people, offering the nation non-partisan leadership virtuously dedicated to the common good.

The ideal of the Patriot President was endangered, the Founding Fathers believed, by twin menaces—factionalism and factionalism's ugly offspring, the demagogue. Party competition would only encourage unscrupulous men to appeal to popular passion and prejudice. Alexander Hamilton in the 71st Federalist bemoaned the plight of the people, "beset as they continually are . . . by the snares of the ambitious, the avaricious, the desperate, by the artifices of men who possess their confidence more than they deserve it, and of those who seek to possess rather than to deserve it."

Pervading the Federalist was a theme sounded explicitly both in the first paper and the last: the fear that unleashing popular passions would bring on "the military despotism of a victorious demagogue." If the "mischiefs of faction" were, James Madison admitted in the Tenth Federalist, "sown in the nature of man," the object of politics was to repress this insidious disposition, not to yield to it. "If I could not go to heaven but with a party," said Thomas Jefferson, "I would not go there at all."

So the Father of his Country in his Farewell Address solemnly warned his countrymen against "the baneful effects of the spirit of party." That spirit, Washington conceded, was "inseparable from our nature"; but for popular government it was "truly their worst enemy." The "alternate domination of one faction over another," Washington said, would lead in the end to "formal and permanent despotism." The spirit of a party, "a fire not to be quenched . . . demands a uniform vigilance to prevent its bursting into a flame, lest, instead of warming, it should consume."

Yet even as Washington called on Americans to "discourage and restrain" the spirit of party, parties were beginning to crystallize around him. The eruption of partisanship in defiance of such august counsel argued that party competition might well serve functional necessities in the democratic republic.

After all, honest disagreement over policy and principle called for candid debate. And parties, it appeared, had vital roles to play in the consummation of the Constitution. The distribution of powers among three equal branches inclined the national government toward a chronic condition of stalemate. Parties offered the means of overcoming the constitutional separation of powers by coordinating the executive and legislative branches and furnishing the connective tissue essential to effective government. As national associations, moreover, parties were a force against provincialism and separatism. As instruments of compromise, they encouraged, within the parties as well as between them, the containment and mediation of national quarrels, at least until slavery broke the parties up. Henry D. Thoreau cared little enough for politics, but he saw the point: "Politics is, as it were, the gizzard of society, full of grit and gravel, and the two political parties are its two opposite halves, which grind on each other."

Furthermore, as the illustrations in these volumes so gloriously remind us, party competition was a great source of entertainment and fun—all the more important in those faraway days before the advent of baseball and football, of movies and radio and television. "To take a hand in the regulation of society and to discuss it," Alexis de Tocqueville observed when he visited America in the 1830s, "is his biggest concern and, so to speak, the only pleasure an American knows. . . . Even the women frequently attend public meetings and listen to political harangues as a recreation from their household labors. Debating clubs are, to a certain extent, a substitute for theatrical entertainments."

Condemned by the Founding Fathers, unknown to the Constitution, parties nonetheless imperiously forced themselves into political life. But the party system rose from the bottom up. For half a century, the first half-dozen Presidents continued to hold themselves above party. The disappearance of the Federalist party after the War of 1812 suspended party competition. James Monroe, with no opponent at all in the election of 1820, presided proudly over the Era of Good Feelings, so called because there were no parties around to excite ill feelings. Monroe's successor, John Quincy Adams, despised electioneering and inveighed against the "fashion of peddling for popularity by traveling around the country gathering crowds together, hawking for public dinners, and spouting empty speeches." Men of the old republic believed presidential candidates should be men who already deserved the people's confidence rather than those seeking to win it. Character and virtue, not charisma and ambition, should be the grounds for choosing a President.

Adams was the last of the old school. Andrew Jackson, by beating him in the 1828 election, legitimized party politics and opened a new political era. The rationale of the new school was provided by Jackson's counselor and successor, Martin Van Buren, the classic philosopher of the role of party in the American democracy. By the time Van Buren took his own oath of office in 1837, parties were entrenched as the instruments of American self-government. In Van Buren's words, party battles "rouse the sluggish to exertion, give increased energy to the most active intellect, excite a salutary vigilance over our public functionaries, and prevent that apathy which has proved the ruin of Republics."

Apathy may indeed have proved the ruin of republics, but rousing the sluggish to exertion proved, ironically, the ruin of Van Buren. The architect of the party system became the first casualty of the razzle-dazzle campaigning the system quickly generated. The Whigs' Tippecanoe-and-Tyler-too campaign of 1840 transmuted the democratic Van Buren into a gilded aristocrat and assured his defeat at the polls. The "peddling for popularity" John Quincy Adams had deplored now became standard for party campaigners.

But the new methods were still forbidden to the presidential candidates themselves. The feeling lingered from earlier days that stumping the country in search of votes was demagoguery beneath the dignity of the presidency. Van Buren's code permitted—indeed expected—parties to inscribe their creed in platforms and candidates to declare their principles in letters published in newspapers. Occasionally candidates—William Henry Harrison in 1840, Winfield Scott in 1852—made a speech, but party surrogates did most of the hard work.

As late as 1858, Van Buren, advising his son John, one of the great popular orators of the time, on the best way to make it to the White House, emphasized the "rule . . . that the people will never make a man President who is so importunate as to show by his life and conversation that he not only has an eye on, but is in active pursuit of the office. . . . No man who has laid himself out for it, and was unwise enough to let the people into his secret, ever yet obtained it. Clay, Calhoun, Webster, Scott, and a host of lesser lights, should serve as a guide-post to future aspirants."

The continuing constraint on personal campaigning by candidates was reinforced by the desire of party managers to present their nominees as all things to all men. In 1835 Nicholas Biddle, the wealthy Philadelphian who had been Jackson's mortal opponent in the famous Bank War, advised the Whigs not to let General Harrison "say one single word about his principles or his creed. . . . Let him say nothing, promise nothing. Let no committee, no convention, no town meeting ever extract from him a single word about what he thinks now, or what he will do hereafter. Let the use of pen and ink be wholly forbidden as if he were a mad poet in Bedlam."

We cherish the memory of the famous debates in 1858 between Abraham Lincoln and Stephen A. Douglas. But those debates were not part of a presidential election. When the presidency was at stake two years later, Lincoln gave no campaign speeches on the issues darkly dividing the country. He even expressed doubt about party platforms—"the formal written platform system," as he called it. The candidate's character and record, Lincoln thought, should constitute his platform: "On just such platforms all our earlier and better Presidents were elected."

However, Douglas, Lincoln's leading opponent in 1860, foreshadowed the future when he broke the sound barrier and dared venture forth on thinly disguised campaign tours. Yet Douglas established no immediate precedent. Indeed, half a dozen years later Lincoln's successor, Andrew Johnson, discredited presidential stumping by his "swing around the circle" in the midterm election of 1866. "His performances in a western tour in advocacy of his own election," commented Benjamin F. Butler, who later led the fight in Congress for Johnson's impeachment, ". . . disgusted everybody." The tenth article of impeachment charged Johnson with bringing "the high office of the President of the United States into contempt, ridicule, and disgrace" by delivering "with a loud voice certain intemperate, inflammatory, and scandalous harangues . . . peculiarly indecent and unbecoming in the Chief Magistrate of the United States."

Though presidential candidates Horatio Seymour in 1868, Rutherford B. Hayes in 1876, and James A. Garfield in 1880 made occasional speeches, only Horace Greeley in 1872, James G. Blaine in 1884, and most spectacularly, William Jennings Bryan in 1896 followed Douglas's audacious example of stumping the country. Such tactics continued to provoke disapproval. Bryan, said John Hay, who had been Lincoln's private secretary and was soon to become McKinley's secretary of state, "is begging for the presidency as a tramp might beg for a pie."

Respectable opinion still preferred the "front porch" campaign, employed by Garfield, by Benjamin Harrison in 1888, and most notably by McKinley in 1896. Here candidates received and addressed numerous delegations at their own homes—a form, as the historian Gil Troy writes, of "stumping in place."

While candidates generally continued to stand on their dignity, popular campaigning in presidential elections flourished in these years, attaining new heights of participation (82 percent of eligible voters in 1876 and never once from 1860 to 1900 under 70 percent) and new wonders of pyrotechnics and ballyhoo. Parties mobilized the electorate as never before, and political iconography was never more ingenious and fantastic. "Politics, considered not as the science of government, but as the art of winning elections and securing office," wrote the keen British observer James Bryce, "has reached in the United States a development surpassing in elaborateness that of England or France as much as the methods of those countries surpass the methods of

Servia or Roumania." Bryce marveled at the "military discipline" of the parties, at "the demonstrations, the parades and receptions, the badges and brass bands and triumphal arches," at the excitement stirred by elections—and at "the disproportion that strikes a European between the merits of the presidential candidate and the blazing enthusiasm which he evokes."

Still the old taboo held back the presidential candidates themselves. Even so irrepressible a campaigner as President Theodore Roosevelt felt obliged to hold his tongue when he ran for reelection in 1904. This unwonted abstinence reminded him, he wrote in considerable frustration, of the July day in 1898 when he was "lying still under shell fire" during the Spanish-American War. "I have continually wished that I could be on the stump myself."

No such constraint inhibited TR, however, when he ran again for the presidency in 1912. Meanwhile, and for the first time, *both* candidates in 1908—Bryan again, and William Howard Taft—actively campaigned for the prize. The duties of the office, on top of the new requirements of campaigning, led Woodrow Wilson to reflect that same year, four years before he himself ran for President, "Men of ordinary physique and discretion cannot be Presidents and live, if the strain be not somehow relieved. We shall be obliged always to be picking our chief magistrates from among wise and prudent athletes,—a small class."

Theodore Roosevelt and Woodrow Wilson combined to legitimate a new conception of presidential candidates as active molders of public opinion in active pursuit of the highest office. Once in the White House, Wilson revived the custom, abandoned by Jefferson, of delivering annual state of the union addresses to Congress in person. In 1916 he became the first incumbent President to stump for his own reelection.

The activist candidate and the bully-pulpit presidency were expressions of the growing democratization of politics. New forms of communication were reconfiguring presidential campaigns. In the nineteenth century the press, far more fiercely partisan then than today, had been the main carrier of political information. In the twentieth century the spread of advertising techniques and the rise of the electronic media—radio, television, computerized public opinion polling—wrought drastic changes in the methodology of politics. In particular the electronic age diminished and now threatens to dissolve the historic role of the party.

The old system had three tiers: the politician at one end; the voter at the other; and the party in between. The party's function was to negotiate between the politician and the voters, interpreting each to the other and providing the link that held the political process together. The electric revolution has substantially abolished the sovereignty of the party. Where once the voter turned to the local party leader to find out whom to support, now he looks at television and makes up his own mind. Where once the politician turned to the local party leader to find out what people are thinking, he now takes a computerized poll.

The electronic era has created a new breed of professional consultants, "handlers," who by the 1980s had taken control of campaigns away from the politicians. The traditional pageantry—rallies, torchlight processions, volunteers, leaflets, billboards, bumper stickers—is now largely a thing of the past. Television replaces the party as the means of mobilizing the voter. And as the party is left to wither on the vine, the presidential candidate becomes more pivotal than ever. We shall see the rise of personalist movements, founded not on historic organizations but on compelling personalities, private fortunes, and popular frustrations. Without the stabilizing influence of parties, American politics would grow angrier, wilder, and more irresponsible.

Things have changed considerably from the austerities of the old republic. Where once voters preferred to call presumably reluctant candidates to the duties of the supreme magistracy and rejected pursuit of the office as evidence of dangerous ambition, now they expect candidates to come to them, explain their views and plead for their support. Where nonpartisan virtue had been the essence, now candidates must prove to voters that they have the requisite "fire in the belly." "'Twud be inth'restin," said Mr. Dooley, ". . . if th' fathers iv th' counthry cud come back an' see what has happened while they've been away. In times past whin ye voted f'r prisident ye didn't vote f'r a man. Ye voted f'r a kind iv a statue that ye'd put up in ye'er own mind on a marble pidistal. Ye nivir heerd iv George Wash'nton goin' around th' counthry distributin' five cint see-gars."

We have reversed the original notion that ambition must be disguised and the office seek the man. Now the man—and soon, one must hope, the woman—seeks the office and does so without guilt or shame or inhibition. This is not necessarily a degradation of democracy. Dropping the disguise is a gain for candor, and personal avowals of convictions and policies may elevate and educate the electorate.

On the other hand, the electronic era has dismally reduced both the intellectual content of campaigns and the attention span of audiences. In the nineteenth century political speeches lasted for a couple of hours and dealt with issues in systematic and exhaustive fashion. Voters drove wagons for miles to hear Webster and Clay, Bryan and Teddy Roosevelt, and felt cheated if the famous orator did not give them their money's worth. Then radio came along and cut political addresses down first to an hour, soon to thirty minutes—still enough time to develop substantive arguments.

But television has shrunk the political talk first to fifteen minutes, now to the sound bite and the thirty-second spot. Advertising agencies today sell candidates with all the cynical contrivance they previously devoted to selling detergents and mouthwash. The result is the debasement of American politics. "The idea that you can merchandise candidates for high office like breakfast cereal," Adlai Stevenson said in 1952, "is the ultimate indignity to the democratic process."

Still Bryce's "intermittent fever" will be upon us every fourth year. We will continue to watch wise if not always prudent athletes in their sprint for the White House, enjoy the quadrennial spectacle and agonize about the outcome.

"The strife of the election," said Lincoln after his reelection in 1864, "is but human-nature practically applied to the facts. What has occurred in this case, must ever recur in similar cases. Human-nature will not change."

Lincoln, as usual, was right. Despite the transformation in political methods there remains a basic continuity in political emotions. "For a long while before the appointed time has come," Tocqueville wrote more than a century and a half ago, "the election becomes the important and, so to speak, the all-engrossing topic of discussion. Factional ardor is redoubled, and all the artificial passions which the imagination can create in a happy and peaceful land are agitated and brought to light. . . .

"As the election draws near, the activity of intrigue and the agitation of the populace increase; the citizens are divided into hostile camps, each of which assumes the name of its favorite candidate; the whole nation glows with feverish excitement; the election is the daily theme of the press, the subject of every private conversation, the end of every thought and every action, the sole interest of the present.

"It is true," Tocqueville added, "that as soon as the choice is determined, this ardor is dispelled, calm returns, and the river, which had nearly broken its banks, sinks to its usual level; but who can refrain from astonishment that such a storm should have arisen?"

The election storm in the end blows fresh and clean. With the tragic exception of 1860, the American people have invariably accepted the result and given the victor their hopes and blessings. For all its flaws and follies, democracy abides.

Let us now turn the pages and watch the gaudy parade of American presidential politics pass by in all its careless glory.

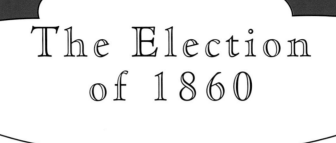

The Election of 1860

William E. Gienapp was educated at Yale University and the University of California, Berkeley, where he received his Ph.D. in 1980. He has taught at the University of California, Berkeley, and the University of Wyoming, and since 1989 has been a member of the history department at Harvard University. A specialist in antebellum politics, he has published a number of essays in books and scholarly journals. His book *The Origins of the Republican Party, 1852–1856* (1987), the first of a projected two-volume study of the party before the Civil War, was co-winner of the Avery O. Craven Prize.

In terms of its consequences, the 1860 presidential election was the most momentous in American history. The campaign preceding the election in November was, in the words of one historian, "a campaign like none other." Among its most unusual features was the fact that there were four major candidates in the field.

The first party to select a standard bearer was the Constitutional Union Party, which was organized expressly for this election. Representing yet another attempt to form a national conservative organization in place of the defunct Whig Party, its convention nominated for president John Bell of Tennessee, a southern moderate. He ran on a platform that simply called for the maintenance of the Constitution, the Union, and the laws.

The sectional controversy of the 1850s had taken its toll on the Democratic Party, and the division now ran so deep that the northern and southern wings could not agree on a candidate. Eventually northern Democrats nominated Senator Stephen A. Douglas of Illinois on a platform upholding the doctrine of popular sovereignty (this was the idea that the residents of a territory should decide whether they wanted slavery or not). The vast majority of southern delegates bolted and nominated Vice President John C. Breckinridge on a platform calling for adoption of a congressional slave code for the territories. In the South, Breckinridge was considered the regular Democratic candidate.

The Republicans surprised veteran party watchers by selecting Abraham Lincoln of Illinois as their presidential nominee. Lincoln had been out of public office for more than a decade, but he had gained national attention from his debates with Douglas in 1858, was acceptable to all factions of the party, and came from a critical state. The delegates concluded that Lincoln was their strongest candidate, and he was nominated on the third ballot.

During the 1860 campaign, mass-produced photographs were sold to the public. In 1859 a process was developed for reproducing inexpensive sheets of tintypes (in smaller forms known as ferrotypes)—hence a new campaign item, photographs of the candidates. There are more than 120 different photographs of Lincoln. This ferrotype promotes the candidates of the Constitutional Union Party, Bell and Everett.

With the Democratic Party divided, Republicans expected to win and, according to one party leader, "everywhere surpassed their opponents in earnestness and enthusiasm." Neither the Bell nor the Breckinridge parties conducted a particularly vigorous campaign. The Republicans and Douglas Democrats were much more energetic since the election would be decided in the North, and only Lincoln and Douglas had any chance of carrying free states. The only hope of defeating Lincoln was that Douglas would take enough northern states to send the election into the House of Representatives. Popular interest remained high despite the election's seemingly foreordained outcome.

To a large extent, campaign techniques in 1860 carried forward those developed in presidential elections since 1840. Parties relied on countless speeches by party orators to bring their message to the voters. Prominent

A Bell and Everett silk ribbon from photographic portraits by Matthew Brady.

Republicans such as William H. Seward and Salmon P. Chase stumped for Lincoln. In the North, a majority of Democratic leaders endorsed Douglas, while in the South they mostly supported Breckinridge (although a few, headed by Alexander H. Stephens of Georgia, backed Douglas). Bell had some prominent supporters, but his campaign failed to attract young men, who traditionally supplied much of the energy and performed the bulk of the labor of a national campaign.

Campaign organizations followed the structure perfected in previous national campaigns. Governor Edwin D. Morgan of New York was chairman of the Republican campaign committee with primary responsibility for raising money, George G. Fogg of New Hampshire served as secretary and ran the speakers' bureau, and Senator Preston King of New York

Carte de visite of Stephen A. Douglas.

supervised the distribution of campaign literature from Washington. The key leaders of the Douglas campaign were Augustus Belmont, who was national chairman and took charge of fund-raising, and Congressman Moses Taylor of Louisiana, who looked after day-to-day affairs mostly from Washington. The Breckinridge campaign was largely run from Washington by a group of party insiders; it was managed by Isaac

Breckinridge-Lane ferrotype set in brass with stickpin on back.

Stevens of Oregon. Congressman Alexander Boteler of Virginia headed the Bell campaign apparatus.

The parties produced campaign documents of various kinds, including biographies of the candidates, congressional speeches, and short tracts written specifically for the election. Most pamphlets were distributed either by party newspapers, the state committee, or a congressional frank-

ing committee in Washington. With the biggest war chest, Republicans were the most active in circulating printed materials. They sent out copies of the Lincoln-Douglas debates of 1858, and Horace Greeley and John F. Cleveland brought together a number of important campaign documents in a *Political Textbook for 1860*, which went through fourteen editions. The power of the Republican juggernaut was demonstrated by the situation in Madison County, Illinois, a rural locality, where the party had disseminated an astonishing six thousand documents by the middle of June.

Several campaign biographies of Lincoln were produced. An early one by Ichabod Codding, an abolitionist,

(Right) Stephen A. Douglas silk ribbon from photographic portrait by Matthew Brady. (Opposite page) Multicolored political chart illustrating the 1860 candidates and the principal issues.

Illinois State Historical Library

Abraham Lincoln formally accepts the Republican Party's nomination, Springfield, Illinois, June 16, 1860. In the detail from the photograph at the left, Lincoln can be seen more clearly, standing upper right.

portrayed Lincoln as an advanced opponent of slavery and was immediately suppressed by nervous Republicans. William Dean Howells wrote a biography; he was later rewarded by appointment as consul in Venice. A life appeared in German, but the most widely circulated campaign biography in 1860, with estimated sales of 200,000 copies, was written by John Locke Scripps. Jointly sponsored by the Chicago *Tribune* and the *New York Tribune* and based partly on material supplied by the candidate, Scripps's 32-page study sold for as little as two cents a copy in large lots. Republican clubs were urged to purchase multiple copies for distribution. The other parties did not go in for campaign biographies, except for a life of Douglas penned by James W. Sheehan of the Chicago *Times*.

Recognizing that naturalized voters were a key element in many northern states, Republicans made special appeals to Germans and other immigrant groups. Besides newspapers, campaign pamphlets, and documents in foreign languages, the party established a special division, headed by the German-American leader Carl Schurz, to coordinate foreign-born orators stumping for Lincoln.

Newspapers remained the primary means of reaching the voters. Most newspapers of this era were highly partisan, and hewed to the party line rather than objectively reporting the news. Republicans surpassed their opponents, both in the number and the quality of

Grand National Banner for Bell and Everett.

The obverse and reverse of 1860 "donut" ferrotypes showing the four presidential and the four vice presidential candidates.

their papers. In the South, the press divided between Bell and Breckinridge, with a few sheets (such as John Forsythe's Mobile *Register*) supporting Douglas. Douglas's campaign was hurt by the absence of a major paper in either New York or Chicago; in the latter city, Cyrus McCormick bought the financially strapped *Times* and promptly swung it away from Douglas. Special journals created for the campaign also appeared. The most famous was *The Rail Splitter*, a Republican sheet printed in Chicago. Published every Saturday, it included the usual partisan editorials and slanted news, along with cartoons, songs, and jokes designed to lampoon the opposition and bring a touch of humor to the campaign. It circulated widely among Republican clubs.

The other standard campaign practice, perfected earlier, was the mass meeting. Throughout the contest, the parties held countless rallies, parades, picnics, barbecues, pole raisings, and other events to attract and entertain the masses. Flags, banners, and likenesses of the candidates decorated buildings and were strung across streets in countless communities. The Breckinridge forces, for example, kicked off their campaign with a large rally in Washington, D.C., featuring a speech by President James Buchanan. And Douglas was greeted by demonstrations in various communities he visited, including Chicago, where downtown buildings were illuminated in his honor and the occasion culminated with a spectacular show of fireworks.

Republicans held a well-publicized meeting in Lincoln's hometown of Springfield in August to ratify his nomination. Thousands of Republicans, including a number from nearby states, flocked to the Illinois capital on foot, on horseback, in wagons, and by specially chartered trains. The buildings in the center of town were decorated with flags, transparencies, and banners. A huge parade stretching some eight miles kicked off the proceedings at ten in the morning. At its head was an immense ball with

Campaign imagery began to appear on cachets, or commemorative envelopes, circa 1856. These 1860 engraved envelopes have slogans and pictures of the candidates.

mottoes such as "The Republican ball is in motion," and "We link-on to Lincoln—our fathers were for Clay." Then came Republican clubs and bands, couples on gaily decorated horses, floats, county and town delegations, and over a hundred wagons hauling celebrants. Wagons and floats were festively decorated and carried signs and prominently displayed various party symbols. Emblazoned with a banner that read "Protection to American Industries," one float even contained a woolen mill making cloth.

After passing Lincoln's home while the candidate watched from the front porch, the procession wound its way to the fairgrounds, where Republicans had erected five stands for the many speakers to address the assembled throng. Constant cheering and singing rent the air. Evening

brought more speeches in town, along with a fireworks display and a torchlight parade past illuminated buildings. "As far as the eye could reach," one newspaper reported, ". . . a seemingly interminable line of flame stretched out its moving length." In all, perhaps fifty thousand people participated in the festivities.

To a much greater degree than in their first national campaign four years earlier, Republicans in 1860 utilized

The campaign ribbon at left and the oil painting, medal, and ribbon on the opposite page show how Abraham Lincoln was presented as the "rail-splitter." The intention of the Republican campaign was to portray Lincoln as a figure with whom ordinary Americans could identify.

Chicago Historical Society

party symbols and exploited campaign pageantry. They emphasized Lincoln's humble origins, portraying the candidate as a self-made man and hence a symbol of democracy. This rail-splitter image began when his cousin John Hanks appeared at the Republican state convention in

Decatur, Illinois, with two rails he claimed to have split with Lincoln in 1830. These objects created a sensation on the floor, and under the direction of Richard Oglesby, an Illinois Republican leader, an industry in Lincoln rails soon developed, as Republican clubs eagerly sought to purchase the genuine article or a close substitute. Banners and transparencies pictured Lincoln in rude western garb with an axe; split rails or a log cabin were often also visible.

Republicans routinely referred to their candidate as Honest Abe, Honest Old Abe, or just Old Abe in order to enhance his image as a common man. This emphasis on Lincoln's personal integrity stood in sharp contrast to Buchanan's sorry record of corruption, and the nickname "Abe" reinforced the image of Lincoln as a humble man of the people. Ironically, Lincoln hated the name and never used it—its almost universal adoption was strictly for campaign purposes.

Party songs were another standard feature of the campaign. Here again, the Republicans outdid their opponents. Campaign songs were a traditional way of rousing enthusiasm and entertaining the faithful, and glee clubs often led the crowd in singing. Most songs contained little ideological content; a thumping melody and some sharp digs at the opposition were what counted. Of all the campaign songs Republicans sang in 1860, none was more popular than "Ain't you glad you joined the Republicans," set to the tune of "The Old Gray Mare." It began:

Old Abe Lincoln came out of the wilderness,
Out of the wilderness,
    out of the wilderness,
Old Abe Lincoln came out of the wilderness,
Down in Illinois.

The chorus went:

Silk ribbons from photographic portraits by Matthew Brady. John Bell (left) and John Breckinridge.

Ain't you glad you joined the Republicans,
Joined the Republicans,
    joined the Republicans,
Ain't you glad you joined the Republicans,
Down in Illinois?

On election night when Lincoln left the Springfield telegraph office once victory was assured, the crowd of Republicans outside spontaneously broke into this song.

Cartoons were an important feature of all four parties' campaigns, although Republicans were again most active in this regard.

Ferrotype pin of Douglas and his wife.

Republican cartoons, and some issued by their opponents, incorporated the symbol of the split rail. Pro-Bell cartoons emphasized the Union issue and the extremism of the other candidates; a particularly well-executed drawing showed the other three candidates ripping the country apart while Bell tried to sew it back together. Both wings of the Democratic Party aggressively exploited the race issue, and party cartoons frequently contained unfavorable images of blacks and ugly racial references. Opponents also routinely portrayed the Republican Party as an extremist organization that threatened the Union. One anti-Lincoln cartoon, issued by Currier and Ives, showed Lincoln sitting on a rail held by Horace Greeley of the *New York Tribune* battering down the door to the lunatic asylum while an assortment of Republicans representing various radical enthusiasms wait to enter.

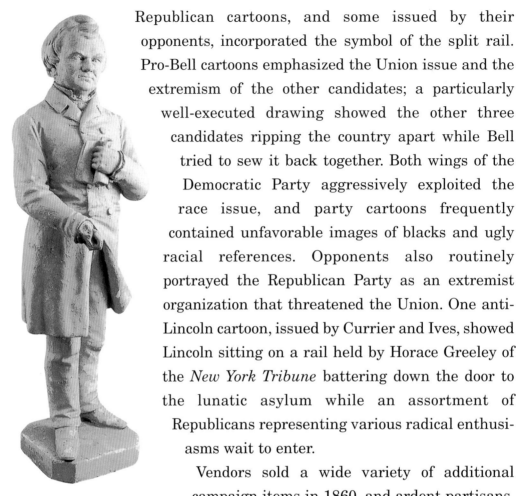

Plaster figurine of Douglas, circa 1860.

Vendors sold a wide variety of additional campaign items in 1860, and ardent partisans, including ladies, wore medals, ribbons, and other trinkets to proclaim their preferences. The well-funded Republicans distributed the largest number of such items. The Republican emphasis on symbols and Lincoln's personality accorded trinkets, visuals, and campaign paraphernalia a central role. Campaign tokens and badges referred to Honest Abe, Republican marchers carried axes, and party stationery displayed a split-rail fence as well as the candidate's visage. These objects sometimes contained references to issues, including slavery extension, the homestead law, the tariff, and the Union.

There are many styles of Lincoln cotton flag banners from this campaign. The Douglas portrait flag banner, however, is an extremely rare item.

Militantly antislavery items seem to have been circulated primarily if not exclusively in rock-ribbed Republican areas. Likewise, items endorsing a protective tariff were particularly used in Pennsylvania and New Jersey, where tariff sentiment was strong.

The Bell and Douglas campaign items emphasized the Union. One Bell token, for example, proclaimed "The Constitution and the Union/Now and Forever," while a campaign ribbon read, "The Union and the Constitution/

Pair of silk ribbons with engraved portraits of Lincoln and Douglas.

One and Inseparable." Douglas items also stressed the Union, but many contained references to Douglas's doctrine of popular sovereignty. One Douglas token, with a rather long inscription, declared, "Popular Sovereignty / Non Intervention by the General Government in Any of the States or Territories of the Union / Let the People of Each Rule." Alone among the candidates, Breckinridge items paid only lip service to the Union, and often coupled references to it with endorsements of southern rights, as for example in the token that said, "Our Rights, the Constitution and the Union." In New Orleans, an enraged mob nearly lynched a dealer of campaign buttons whose stock mistakenly included a Lincoln medal.

The major innovation of the Douglas campaign was an extensive speaking tour by the candidate. Before the Civil War presidential candidates, respecting the popular belief that it was improper to seek the office, traditionally did not campaign in person. Douglas initially announced his intention to follow this precedent, but facing an uphill battle, he changed his mind. His extensive speaking tour was unprecedented and in many ways foreshadowed modern presidential campaigns. Accompanied by his vivacious wife, who remained at his side throughout the campaign, Douglas left New York City in July under the guise of traveling to see his mother in upstate New York and visit his boyhood home in Vermont. Douglas's trip fooled no one. From railroad platforms, hotel balconies, and other locations he delivered a series of political speeches warning that the Union was in peril. Tracing his circuitous route, the Republican press lampooned the candidate's "maternal pilgrimage" and circulated a broadside requesting information on the "lost" son.

Following his swing across New England, Douglas traveled through the upper South, emphasizing the Union issue and attacking the Breckinridge faction as disunionists. After a brief stop in New York City, he was off again, this time heading west. On September 15, two months after he had started, he was finally reunited with his mother. He then pushed across upstate New York and into the western states, delivering another series of political addresses along the way. When the October state elections in Pennsylvania, Indiana, and Ohio unmistakably indicated that Lincoln would be elected in November, the Illinois senator, defying threats to his personal safety, entered the deep South, speaking in Tennessee, Alabama, and Georgia. He continued to attack disunionists in the South, and as he had done earlier, denied that Lincoln's election would justify secession. The Little Giant finished his strenuous three-and-a-half month campaign, during which he had spoken almost every day, on election eve in Mobile. He had visited twenty-three states in the Northeast, the Northwest, the upper South, and the deep South, and in the process broken his health.

Wide-Awakes were ardent Lincoln supporters who paraded along military lines. Over their suits they wore kepis and capes.

In contrast to Douglas, Lincoln did not campaign in 1860. Adopting the time-honored stance of presidential candidates, Lincoln told one supporter, "By the lesson of the past, and the united voice of all discreet friends, I am neither [to] write or speak a word for the public." Setting up shop in the governor's room in the State House, he greeted visitors but said nothing of consequence. In fact, Lincoln was the least active of the four candidates and the only one who did not make a single speech.

Instead, the major innovation of the Republican Party in the 1860 campaign was the Wide-Awake society. Marching clubs had appeared in earlier campaigns, but never on the scale or with such fanfare as the Wide-Awakes. The first Wide-Awake club had been formed in Hartford in February 1860, for the state election. The concept caught on, and in the summer of 1860 similar societies, also taking the name Wide-Awakes, were organized throughout the North. Communities wishing to organize

Centerfold wood-block print from *Harper's Weekly* illustrating a Wide-Awake torchlight parade in New York City, October 3, 1860.

official Wide-Awake societies were instructed to contact the Hartford club for information.

Made up mostly of young men, the Wide-Awakes were a Republican marching organization. Members sang campaign songs, shouted party chants, cheered and marched in Republican parades. Members also did much of the onerous daily work, such as distributing literature, putting up hand-bills, and compiling voter lists. Their uniform was made up of a military hat, glazed cape (to protect them from the oil drippings), and an oil lamp or torch, usually

Milkglass plaque of Lincoln.

mounted on a rail and often decorated with a flag emblazoned with Lincoln's name. Enterprising merchants sold complete uniforms for $1.15 or more. It has been estimated that there were 400,000 Wide-Awakes in 1860. In the West, they sometimes took the name "Rail Splitters" or "Rail Maulers."

Members were organized along military lines with officers and privates. At night with their torches blazing they presented a spectacular sight. Officers carried different colored lanterns depicting their rank. They practiced intricate marching steps to entertain spectators, including a zig-zag maneuver that imitated a split-rail fence. Most clubs had a band that played martial music and campaign tunes, and as they marched, members sang campaign tunes and shouted partisan chants in unison.

The popularity of the Wide-Awakes prompted opponents to emulate their example. The Douglas forces organized the "Ever Readys," "Little Giants," and "Douglas Invincibles." The Bell organization followed suit with the "Bell Ringers," "Minute Men," and "Union Sentinels"; these clubs often carried bells as well as torches. Even the Breckinridge forces, though

THE GREAT UNION TORCHLIGHT PROCESSION IN NEW YORK, ON THE 23RD OF OCTOBER, 1860.—NO. 1. CAPTAIN RYNDERS' POCKET PIECE.—NO. 2. FULL RIGGED SHIP, DRAWN BY TEN HORSES.— HORACE GREELEY AND A DARK-COLORED YOUNG LADY.—NO. 4 KNIGHTS OF THE UNION AND TEMPLE OF LIBERTY.—SEE PAGE 368.

GREAT UNION TORCHLIGHT PROCESSION IN NEW YORK—EMBLEMS IN THE FIRST DIVISION.—NO. 1. WAGON WITH INSCRIPTIONS OF YOUNG MEN'S INDEPENDENT CLUB.—NO. 2. A FAST SPECIMEN AMERICA.—NO. 3. TRUCK BEARING INSCRIPTION AND SHIELDS OF THE THIRTEEN STATES.—SEE PAGE 368.

not numerous in the North, marched as "National Democratic Volunteers." None of these rival societies, however, attracted anywhere near the publicity or membership of the Wide-Awakes. Nor could they match the enthusiasm of the confident Republicans. At least one Republican campaign cartoon portrayed Lincoln as a Wide-Awake, alertly preventing his opponents from breaking into the White House.

A monstrous Wide-Awake parade was held in New York City in October, shortly before the election. Republicans claimed that 100,000 people witnessed what they called a rally of banners of light. Spectators jammed Broadway as an estimated ten thousand Wide-Awakes marched in steady cadence, their lamps blazing, while rockets and roman candles roared from the rooftops across the sky. The martial music, spectacle of light, and rhythmic tread of the marchers mingled with cheers of spectators to produce a powerful impression.

Stimulated by the Republicans' pageantry and Douglas's speaking tour, the turnout was only slightly below that of 1856. Lincoln ran first among the four candidates but with less than 40 percent of the popular vote failed to gain a majority. He easily outdistanced his rivals in the electoral college, however, winning 180 electoral votes. Because of his strength in the heavily populated North, he was elected even though he did not carry a single southern state and had virtually no support in that region outside the border states. Even if the votes for Douglas, Bell, and Breckinridge had been combined behind a single candidate, Lincoln still would have won.

Aided by effective symbols such as the rail-splitter image and the Wide-Awake Society, Republicans had managed to carry their first national election. In response to Lincoln's victory, the states of the deep South seceded from the Union, and in April 1861, six weeks after he was inaugurated the first Republican president in American history, the Civil War began.

Opposite page: the great Union torchlight parade, New York City, October 23, 1860.

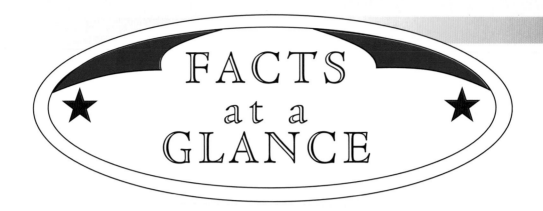

FACTS at a GLANCE

ABRAHAM LINCOLN

- **Born:** February 12, 1809, in Hardin County, Kentucky
- **Parents:** Thomas and Nancy Hanks Lincoln
- **Education:** no formal education
- **Occupation:** Lawyer
- **Married:** Mary Todd (1818–1882) on November 4, 1842
- **Children:** Robert Todd Lincoln (1843–1926); Edward Baker Lincoln (1846–1850); William Wallace Lincoln (1850–1862); Thomas "Tad" Lincoln (1853–1871)
- **Died:** April 15, 1865, at Petersen's Boarding House in Washington, D.C.

Served as the 16TH PRESIDENT OF THE UNITED STATES,
- March 4, 1861, to April 15, 1865

VICE PRESIDENT
- Hannibal Hamlin, 1861–65
- Andrew Johnson, 1865

This fine silk ribbon features Brady portraits of Lincoln and Hamlin.

CABINET

Secretary of State

- William H. Seward (1861–65)

Secretary of the Treasury

- Salmon P. Chase (1861–64)
- William P. Fessenden (1864–65)
- Hugh McCulloch (1865)

Secretary of War

- Simon Cameron (1861–62)
- Edward M. Stanton (1862–65)

Attorney General

- Edward Bates (1861–64)
- James Speed (1864–65)

Postmaster General

- Montgomery Blair (1861–64)
- William Dennison (1864–65)

Secretary of the Navy

- Gideon Welles (1861–65)

Secretary of the Interior

- Caleb B. Smith (1861–63)
- John P. Usher (1863–65)

POLITICAL POSITIONS

- Member of the Illinois State Legislature, 1834–1842

- Member of the U.S. House of Representatives, 1847–1849

- President of the United States, 1861–1865

NOTABLE EVENTS DURING LINCOLN'S ADMINISTRATION

1860   On November 6, Lincoln is elected president of the United States; in December, the legislature of South Carolina votes to leave the Union. Other Southern states follow, forming the Confederate States of America.

1861   Lincoln is sworn in as president March 4; Confederates fire on Fort Sumter in Charleston harbor, South Carolina, on April 12, beginning the Civil War.

1863   Lincoln's Emancipation Proclamation frees slaves in the rebellious states; Union forces under General George G. Meade force the Army of Northern Virginia to turn back after three days of fighting at Gettysburg, July 1–3; in the west, the important city of Vicksburg falls to Union troops under General Ulysses S. Grant on July 4; Lincoln outlines his plan for reconstruction.

1864   General William T. Sherman begins his "March to the Sea" through Atlanta; Lincoln is reelected as president, winning 212 out of 223 possible electoral votes and 55 percent of the popular vote.

1865   On March 4, Lincoln delivers his second inaugural address, urging the people to "bind up the nation's wounds"; General Lee surrenders to General Grant at Appomattox Court House April 9; while watching the play "Our American Cousin" at Ford's Theater in Washington, D.C., Lincoln is shot by Confederate sympathizer John Wilkes Booth on April 14; Lincoln dies at 7:55 A.M. April 15.

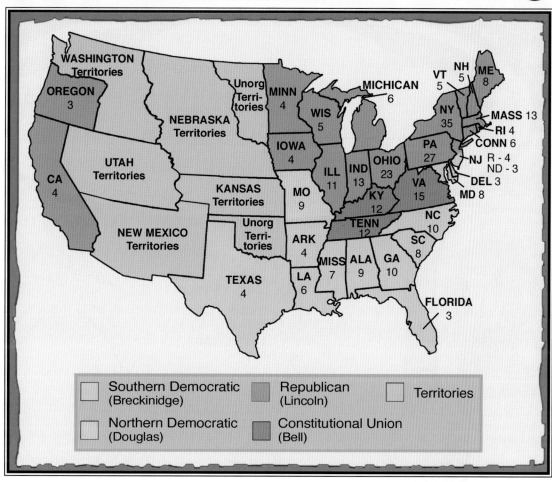

WASHINGTON
Territories

OREGON
3

Unorg
Terri-
tories

MINN
4

MICHICAN
6

VT
5

NH
5

ME
8

NEBRASKA
Territories

WIS
5

NY
35

MASS 13

RI 4

UTAH
Territories

IOWA
4

PA
27

CONN 6

NJ R - 4
ND - 3

CA
4

KANSAS
Territories

ILL
11

IND
13

OHIO
23

VA
15

DEL 3

MD 8

MO
9

KY
12

NEW MEXICO
Territories

Unorg
Terri-
tories

ARK
4

TENN
12

NC
10

SC
8

TEXAS
4

LA
6

MISS
7

ALA
9

GA
10

FLORIDA
3

| Southern Democratic (Breckinidge) | Republican (Lincoln) | Territories |
| Northern Democratic (Douglas) | Constitutional Union (Bell) | |

Abraham Lincoln managed to win the election of 1860 without capturing the electoral vote of a single Southern state. However, the greater population of the northern states was enough to give Lincoln an easy victory in the electoral college. The Republican candidate received 39.8 percent of the total popular vote, and 180 of the 303 electoral votes. Of the Democrats, Stephen A. Douglas won a greater number of votes than did John C. Breckinridge; Douglas gained 29.5 percent of the national vote to just 18.1 percent by Breckinridge. However, Breckinridge won the electoral votes of most of the Southern states, outpolling Douglas in the electoral college 72 to 12. John Bell also received more electoral votes (39) than Douglas, winning three states—Virginia, Kentucky, and Tennessee. Nationally, the Constitutional Union Party candidate won 12.6 percent of the popular vote.

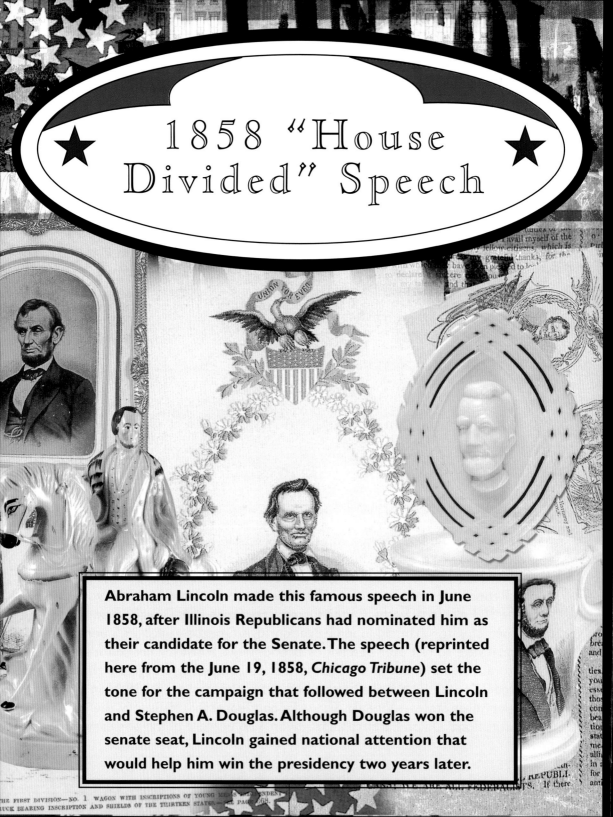

1858 "House Divided" Speech

Abraham Lincoln made this famous speech in June 1858, after Illinois Republicans had nominated him as their candidate for the Senate. The speech (reprinted here from the June 19, 1858, *Chicago Tribune*) set the tone for the campaign that followed between Lincoln and Stephen A. Douglas. Although Douglas won the senate seat, Lincoln gained national attention that would help him win the presidency two years later.

If we could first know where we are, and whither we are tending, we could better judge what to do, and how to do it.

We are now far into the fifth year since a policy was initiated with the avowed object and confident promise of putting and end to slavery agitation. Under the operation of that policy, that agitation has not only not ceased, but has constantly augmented.

In my opinion, it will not cease, until a crisis shall have been reached and passed.

"A house divided against itself cannot stand."

I believe this government cannot endure permanently half slave and half free.

I do not expect the Union to be dissolved—I do not expect the house to fall—but I do expect it will cease to be divided. It will become all one thing, or all the other.

Either the opponents of slavery will arrest the further spread of it, and place it where the public mind shall rest in the belief that it is in the course of ultimate extinction; or its advocates will push it forward till it shall become alike lawful in all the States, old as well as new, North as well as South.

Have we no tendency to the latter condition?

Let any one who doubts carefully contemplate that now almost complete legal combination—piece of machinery, so to speak—compounded of the Nebraska doctrine and the Dred Scott decision. Let him consider not only what work the machinery is adapted to do, and how well adapted; but also let him study the history of its construction, and trace, if he can, or rather fail, if he can, to trace the evidences of design and concert of action among its chief architects, from the beginning. [. . .]

The new year of 1854 found slavery excluded from more than half the States by State constitutions, and from most of the national territory by congressional prohibition. Four days later commenced the struggle which ended in repealing that congressional prohibition. This opened all the national territory to slavery, and was the first point gained.

This necessity had not been overlooked, but had been provided for, as well as might be, in the notable argument of "squatter sovereignty," otherwise called "sacred right of self-government," which latter phrase, though expressive of the only rightful basis of any government, was so perverted in this attempted use of it as to amount to just this: That if any one man choose to enslave another, no third man shall be allowed to object.

That argument was incorporated into the Nebraska bill itself, in the language which follows:

> It being the true intent and meaning of this act not to legislate slavery into any Territory or state, not exclude it therefrom; but to leave the people thereof perfectly free to forl and regulate their domestic institutions in their own way, subject only to the Constitution of the United States.

Then opened the roar of loose declamation in favor of "squatter sovereignty" and "sacred right of self-government."

"But," said opposition members, "let be more specific—let us amend the bill so as to expressly declare that the people of the Territory may exclude slavery." "Not we," said the friends of the measure; and down they voted the amendment.

While the Nebraska Bill was passing through Congress, a law case involving the question of a negro's freedom, by reason of his owner having voluntarily taken him first into a free State and then into a territory covered by the congressional prohibition, and held him as a slave for a long time in each, was passing through the U.S. Circuit Court for the District of Missouri; and both Nebraska bill and lawsuit were brought to a decision in the same month of May, 1854. The negro's name was Dred Scott, which name now designates the decision finally made in the case.

Before the then next Presidential election, the law case came to and was argued in the Supreme Court of the United States; but the decision of it was deferred until after the election. Still, before the election, Senator Trumbull, on the floor of the Senate, requests the leading advocate of the Nebraska bill to state his opinion whether the people of a territory can constitutionally exclude slavery from their limits; and the latter answers, "That is a question for the Supreme Court."

The election came. Mr. Buchanan was elected, and the indorsement, such as it was, secured. That was the second point gained. The indorsment, however, fell short of a clear popular majority by nearly four hundred thousand votes, and so, perhaps, was not overwhelmingly reliable and satisfactory.

The outgoing President, in his last annual message, as impressively as possible echoed back upon the people the weight and authority of the indorsement.

The Supreme Court met again; did not announce their decision, but ordered a reargument.

The Presidential inauguration came, and still no decision of the Court; but the incoming President, in his inaugural address, fervently exhorted the people to abide by the forthcoming decision, whatever it might be.

Then, in a few days, came the decision.

The reputed author of the Nebraska Bill finds an early occasion to make a speech at this capital indorsing the Dred Scott Decision, and vehemently denouncing all opposition to it.

The new President, too, seizes the early occasion of the Silliman letter to indorse and strongly construe that decision, and to express his astonishment that any different view had ever been entertained!

At length a squabble springs up between the President and the author of the Nebraska Bill, on the mere question of fact, whether the Lecompton constitution was or was not, in any just sense, made by the people of Kansas; and in that quarrel the latter declares that all he wants is a fair vote for the people, and that he cares not whether slavery be voted down or voted up. I do not understand his declaration that he cares not whether slavery be voted down or voted up, to be intended by him other than as an apt definition of the policy he would impress upon the public mind—the principle for which he declares he has suffered so much, and is ready to suffer to the end.

And well may he cling to that principle. If he has any parental feeling, well may he cling to it. That principle, is the only shred left of his original Nebraska doctrine. Under the Dred Scott Decision, "squatter sovereignty" squatted out of existence, tumbled down like temporary scaffolding—like the mold at the foundry, served through one blast and fell back into loose sand—helped to carry an election, and then was kicked to the winds. His late joint struggle with the Republicans, against the Lecompton Constitution, involves nothing of the original Nebraska doctrine. That struggle was made on a point, the right of a people to make their own constitution, upon which he and the Republicans have never differed.

The several points of the Dred Scott Decision, in connection with Senator Douglas's "care not" policy, constitute the piece of machinery, in its present state of advancement. This was the third point gained.

The working points of that machinery are:

First, that no Negro slave, imported as such from Africa, and no descendant of such slave can ever be a citizen of any State, in the sense of that term as used in the Constitution of the United States.

This point is made in order to deprive the Negro, in every possible event, of the benefit of this provision of the United States Constitution, which declares that—

"The citizens of each State shall be entitled to all privileges and immunities of citizens in the several States."

Secondly, that "subject to the Constitution of the United States," neither Congress nor a Territorial Legislature can exclude slavery from any United States territory.

This point is made in order that individual men may fill up the territories with slaves, without danger of losing them as property, and thus to enhance the chances of permanency to the institution through all the future.

We cannot absolutely know that all these exact adaptations are the result of preconcert. But when we see a lot of framed timbers, different portions of which we know have been gotten out at different times and places and by different workmen—Stephen, Franklin, Roger and James, for instance—and we see these timbers joined together, and see they exactly make the frame of a house or a mill, all the tenons and mortises exactly fitting, and all the lengths and proportions of the different pieces exactly adapted to their respective places, and not a piece too many or too few, not omitting even scaffolding—or, if a single piece be lacking, we see the place in the frame exactly fitted and prepared yet to bring such piece in—in such a case we find it impossible not to believe that Stephen and Franklin and Roger and James all understood one another from the beginning, and all worked upon a common plan or draft drawn up before the first blow was struck. [. . .]

Our cause, then, must be intrusted to, and conducted by, its own undoubted friends—those whose hands are free, whose hearts are in the work, who do care for the result. Two years ago the Republicans of the nation mustered over thirteen hundred thousand strong. We did this under the single impulse of resistance to a common danger, with every external circumstance against us. Of strange, discordant, and even hostile elements, we gathered from the four winds, and formed and fought the battle through, under the constant hot fire of a disciplined, proud, and pampered enemy. Did we brave all then to falter now?—now when that same enemy is wavering, dissevered, and belligerent? The result is not doubtful. We shall not fail—if we stand firm, we shall not fail. Wise counsels may accelerate or mistakes delay it, but, sooner or later, the victory is sure to come.

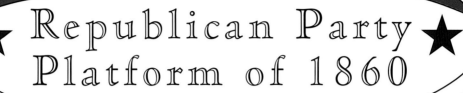

★ Republican Party ★
Platform of 1860

The skillfully written 1860 Republican platform was calculated to win support in the East as well as the West, from conservatives as well as radicals. It reaffirmed the principles of the Declaration of Independence, the Wilmot Proviso (which stated that slavery would not be allowed in any area obtained from Mexico), and the right of each state to control its domestic institutions. It supported internal improvements, a railroad to the Pacific, a homestead law, and a liberal immigration policy. Its reference to tariff adjustment which would "encourage the development of the industrial interests of the whole country" was interpreted as support of a protective tariff, a leading issue in the doubtful states of Pennsylvania and New Jersey. The platform also denied the authority of Congress or a territorial legislature to give legal status to slavery in the territories.

Resolved, That we, the delegated representatives of the Republican electors of the United States [. . .] unite in the following declarations:

1. That the history of the nation, during the last four years, has fully established the propriety and necessity of the organization and perpetuation of the Republican party, and that the causes which called it into existence are permanent in their nature, and now, more than ever before, demand its peaceful and constitutional triumph.

2. That the maintenance of the principles promulgated in the Declaration of Independence and embodied in the Federal Constitution, "That all men are created equal; that they are endowed by their Creator with certain inalienable rights; that among these are life, liberty, and the pursuit of happiness; that to secure these rights, governments are instituted among men, deriving their just powers from the consent of the governed," is essential to the preservation of our Republican institutions; and that the Federal Constitution, the Rights of the States, and the Union of the States, must and shall be preserved.

3. That to the Union of the States this nation owes its unprecedented increase in population, its surprising development of material resources, its rapid augmentation of wealth, its happiness at home and its honor abroad; and we hold in abhorrence all schemes for Disunion, come from whatever source they may: And we congratulate the country that no Republican member of Congress has uttered or countenanced the threats of Disunion so often made by Democratic members without rebuke and with applause from their political associates; and we denounce those threats of Disunion, in case of a popular overthrow of their ascendency, as denying the vital principles of a free government, and as an avowal of contemplated treason, which it is the imperative duty of an indignant People sternly to rebuke and forever silence.

4. That the maintenance inviolate of the rights of the States, and espe-

cially the right of each State to order and control its own domestic institutions according to its own judgment exclusively, is essential to that balance of powers on which the perfection and endurance of our political fabric depends; and we denounce the lawless invasion by armed force of the soil of any State or Territory, no matter under what pretext, as among the gravest of crimes.

5. That the present Democratic Administration has far exceeded our worst apprehensions, in its measureless subserviency to the exactions of a sectional interest, as especially evinced in its desperate exertions to force the infamous Lecompton Constitution upon the protesting people of Kansas; in construing the personal relation between master and servant to involve an unqualified property in persons; in its attempted enforcement, everywhere, on land and sea, through the intervention of Congress and of the Federal Courts of the extreme pretensions of a purely local interest; and in its general and unvarying abuse of the power intrusted to it by a confiding people.

6. That the people justly view with alarm the reckless extravagance which pervades every department of the Federal Government; that a return to rigid economy and accountability is indispensible to arrest the systematic plunder of the public treasury by favored partisans, while the recent startling developments of frauds and corruptions at the Federal metropolis, show that an entire change of administration is imperatively demanded.

7. That the new dogma, that the Constitution, of its own force, carries Slavery into any or all of the Territories of the United States, is a dangerous political heresy, at variance with the explicit provisions of that instrument itself, with contemporaneous exposition, and with legislative and judicial precedent; is revolutionary in its tendency, and subversive of the peace and harmony of the country.

8. That the normal condition of all the territory of the United States is that of freedom; That as our Republican fathers, when they had abolished Slavery in all our national territory, ordained that "no person should be deprived of life, liberty, or property, without due process of law," it becomes our duty, by

legislation, whenever such legislation is necessary, to maintain this provision of the Constitution against all attempts to violate it; and we deny the authority of Congress, of a territorial legislature, or of any individuals, to give legal existence to Slavery in any Territory of the United States.

9. That we brand the recent re-opening of the African slave-trade, under the cover of our national flag, aided by perversions of judicial power, as a crime against humanity and a burning shame to our country and age; and we call upon Congress to take prompt and efficient measures for the total and final suppression of that execrable traffic.

10. That in the recent vetoes, by their Federal Governors, of the acts of the Legislatures of Kansas and Nebraska, prohibiting Slavery in those Territories, we find a practical illustration of the boasted Democratic principle of Non-Intervention and Popular Sovereignty, embodied in the Kansas-Nebraska bill, and a demonstration of the deception and fraud involved therein.

11. That Kansas should, of right, be immediately admitted as a State under the Constitution recently formed and adopted by her people, and accepted by the House of Representatives.

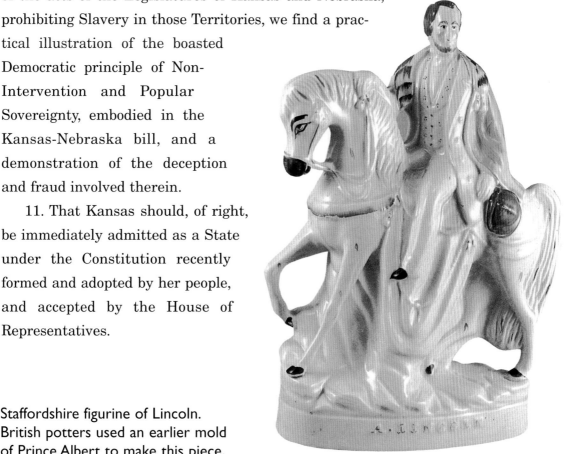

Staffordshire figurine of Lincoln. British potters used an earlier mold of Prince Albert to make this piece.

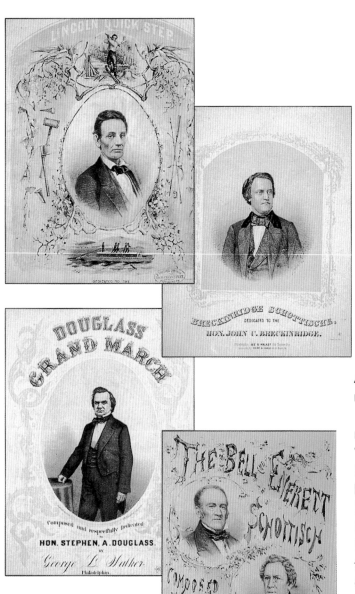

A variety of campaign sheet music from the 1860 election.

The Republican Party did not receive the nickname "Grand Old Party" until 1888. Previously, the nickname had been used by Southern Democrats. When the Republicans won back the Presidency and Congress for the first time since 1876, the *Chicago Tribune* proclaimed: "Let us be thankful that under the rule of the Grand Old Party . . . these United States will resume the onward and upward march which the election of Grover Cleveland in 1884 partially arrested."

12. That, while providing revenue for the support of the General Government by duties upon imports, sound policy requires such an adjustment of these imposts as to encourage the development of the industrial interest of the whole country; and we commend that policy of national exchanges which secures to the working men liberal wages, to agriculture renumerative prices, to mechanics and manufactures an adequate reward for their skill, labor, and enterprise, and to the nation commercial prosperity and independence.

13. That we protest against any sale or alienation to others of the Public Lands held by actual settlers, and against any view of he Homestead policy which regards the settlers as paupers or suppliants for public bounty; and we demand the passage by Congress of the complete and satisfactory Homestead measure which has already passed the House.

14. That the Republican party is opposed to any change in our Naturalization Laws or any State legislation by which the rights of citizenship hitherto accorded to immigrants from foreign lands shall be abridged or impaired; and in favor of giving a full and efficient protection to the rights of all classes of citizens, whether native or naturalized, both at home and abroad.

15. That appropriations by Congress for River and Harbor improvements of a National character, required for the accommodation and security of an existing commerce, are authorized by the Constitution, and justified by the obligations of Government to protect the lives and property of its citizens.

16. That a Railroad to the Pacific Ocean is imperatively demanded by the interest of the whole country; that the Federal Government ought to render immediate and efficient aid in its construction; and that, as preliminary thereto, a daily Overland Mail should be promply established.

17. Finally, having thus set forth our distinctive principles and views, we invite the coöperation of all citizens, however differing on other questions, who substantially agree with us in their affirmance and support.

★ Democratic Party Platforms ★

In 1860 the issue of slavery split the Democratic Party. Northern Democrats nominated Stephen A. Douglas, the junior senator from Illinois. Their platform supported the doctrine of "popular sovereignty"—the idea that voting residents of a territory should decide to allow slavery or not. Southern Democrats united behind John C. Breckinridge, the incumbent vice president. Their platform called for federal protection of property, including slaves, in the territories. The 1860 platforms of both factions of the Democratic Party are reprinted here.

PLATFORM OF THE DOUGLAS DEMOCRATS

1. Resolved, That we, the Democracy of the Union in Convention assembled, hereby declare our affirmance of the resolutions unanimously adopted and declared as a platform of principles by the Democratic convention at Cincinnati, in the year 1856, believing that Democratic principles are unchangeable in their nature, when applied to the same subject matters; and we recommend, as the only further resolutions, the following:

2. Inasmuch as difference of opinion exists in the Democratic party as to the nature and extent of the powers of a Territorial Legislature, and as to the powers and duties of Congress, under the Constitution of the United States, over the institution of slavery within the Territories,

Resolved, That the Democratic party will abide by the decision of the Supreme Court of the United States upon these questions of Constitutional law.

3. Resolved, That it is the duty of the United States to afford ample and complete protection to all its citizens, whether at home or abroad, and whether native or foreign born.

4. Resolved, That one of the necessities of the age, in a military, commercial, and postal point of view, is speedy communication between the Atlantic and Pacific States; and the Democratic party pledge such Constitutional Government aid as will insure the construction of a Railroad to the Pacific coast, at the earliest practicable period.

5. Resolved, That the Democratic party are in favor of the acquisition of the Island of Cuba on such terms as shall be honorable to ourselves and just to Spain.

6. Resolved, That the enactments of the State Legislatures to defeat the faithful execution of the Fugitive Slave Law, are hostile in character,

subversive of the Constitution, and revolutionary in their effect.

7. Resolved, That it is in accordance with the interpretation of the Cincinnati platform, that during the existence of the Territorial Governments the measure of restriction, whatever it may be, imposed by the Federal Constitution on the power of the Territorial Legislature over the subject of the domestic relations, as the same has been, or shall hereafter be finally determined by the Supreme Court of the United States, should be respected by all good citizens, and enforced with promptness and fidelity by every branch of the general government.

PLATFORM OF THE BRECKINRIDGE FACTION

RESOLVED, That the platform adopted by the Democratic party at Cincinnati be affirmed, with the following explanatory resolutions:

1. That the Government of a Territory organized by an act of Congress is provisional and temporary, and during its existence all citizens of the United States have an equal right to settle with their property in the Territory, without their rights, either of person or property, being destroyed or impaired by Congressional or Territorial legislation.

2. That it is the duty of the Federal Government, in all its departments, to protect, when necessary, the rights of persons and property in the Territories, and wherever else its constitutional authority extends.

3. That when the settlers in a Territory, having an adequate population, form a State Constitution, the right of sovereignty commences, and being consummated by admission into the Union, they stand on an equal footing with the people of other States, and the State thus organized ought to be admitted into the Federal Union, whether its constitution prohibits or recognizes the institution of slavery.

Resolved, That the Democratic party are in favor of the acquisition of the Island of Cuba, on such terms as shall be honorable to ourselves and just to Spain, at the earliest practicable moment.

Resolved, That the enactments of State Legislatures to defeat the faithful execution of the Fugitive Slave Law are hostile in character, subversive of the Constitution, and revolutionary in their effect.

Resolved, That the Democracy of the United States recognize it as the imperative duty of this Government to protect the naturalized citizen in all his rights, whether at home or in foreign lands, to the same extent as its native-born citizens.

WHEREAS, One of the greatest necessities of the age, in a political, commercial, postal and military point of view, is speedy communication between the Atlantic and Pacific coasts. Therefore be it

RESOLVED, that the National Democratic party do hereby pledge themselves to use every means in their power to secure the passage of some bill, to the extent of the constitutional authority of Congress, for the construction of a Pacific Railroad from the Mississippi River to the Pacific Ocean, at the earliest practicable moment.

Constitutional Union Platform

In May 1860, former Whigs and moderate men of both the North and South held a convention of what they called the Constitutional Union Party. They nominated Senator John Bell of Tennessee for President and Edward Everett of Massachusetts for Vice President. They avowed no political principle other than the Constitution, the Union, and the enforcement of the laws. This attempt to create a middle-of-the-road party, pledged to solve the slavery issue by reason rather than violence, failed.

Whereas, Experience has demonstrated that Platforms adopted by the partisan Conventions of the country have had the effect to mislead and deceive the people, and at the same time to widen the political divisions of the country, by the creation and encouragement of geographical and sectional parties; therefore

Resolved, that it is both the part of patriotism and of duty to recognize no political principle other than THE CONSTITUTION OF THE COUNTRY, THE UNION OF THE STATES, AND THE ENFORCEMENT OF THE LAWS, and that, as representatives of the Constitutional Union men of the country, in National Convention assembled, we hereby pledge ourselves to maintain, protect, and defend, separately and unitedly, these great principles of public liberty and national safety, against all enemies, at home and abroad; believing that thereby peace may once more be restored to the country; the rights of the People and of the States re-established, and the Government again placed in that condition of justice, fraternity and equality, which, under the example and Constitution of our fathers, has solemnly bound every citizen of the United States to maintain a more perfect union, establish justice, insure domestic tranquillity, provide for the common defense, promote the general welfare, and secure the blessings of liberty to ourselves and our posterity.

The Crittenden Compromise

On December 18, 1860, two days before South
Carolina seceded from the Union, Senator John J.
Crittenden of Kentucky, a most distinguished
statesman, proposed a compromise to avoid civil war.
The Union had been preserved previously through
compromises on the issue of slavery: the Missouri
Compromise (1820), the Compromise of 1850; and
the Kansas-Nebraska Act (1854). In fact, the
Constitution of the United States contains several
"compromises" between the states over slavery.
Crittenden's measures were discussed in committee
for two months in the hope that they might at least
keep the border states in the Union. This sincere but
futile attempt to stop the secession landslide failed.

WHEREAS serious and alarming dissensions have arisen between the northern and southern states, concerning the rights and security of the rights of the slaveholding States, and especially their rights in the common territory of the United States; and whereas it is eminently desirable and proper that these dissensions, which now threaten the very existence of this Union, should be permanently quieted and settled by constitutional provisions, which shall do equal justice to all sections, and thereby restore to all the people that peace and good-will which ought to prevail between all the citizens of the United States: Therefore,

RESOLVED by the Senate and House of Representatives of the United States of America in Congress assembled, (two thirds of both Houses concurring,) That the following articles be, and are hereby, proposed and submitted as amendments to the Constitution of the United States, which shall be valid to all intents and purposes, as part of said Constitution, when ratified by conventions of three-fourths of the several States:

Article 1: In all the territory of the United States now held, or hereafter acquired, situate north of 36 degrees 30 minutes, slavery or involuntary servitude, except as a punishment for crime, is prohibited while such territory shall remain under territorial government. In all the territory south of said line of latitude, slavery of the African race is hereby recognized as existing, and shall not be interfered with by Congress, but shall be protected as property by all the departments of the territorial government during its continuance. And when any territory, north or south of said line, within such boundaries as Congress may prescribe, shall contain the population requisite for a member of Congress according to the then Federal ratio of representation of the people of the United States, it shall, if its form of government be republican, be admitted into the Union, on an equal footing with the original States, with or without slavery, as the constitution of such new State may provide.

Article 2: Congress shall have no power to abolish slavery in places under its exclusive jurisdiction, and situate within the limits of States that permit the holding of slaves.

Article 3: Congress shall have no power to abolish slavery within the District of Columbia, so long as it exists in the adjoining States of Virginia and Maryland, or either, nor without the consent of the inhabitants, nor without just compensation first made to such owners of slaves as do not consent to such abolishment. Nor shall Congress at any time prohibit officers of the Federal Government, or members of Congress, whose duties require them to be in said District, from bringing with them their slaves, and holding them as such during the time their duties may require them to remain there, and afterwards taking them from the District.

Article 4: Congress shall have no power to prohibit or hinder the transportation of slaves from one State to another, or to a Territory, in which slaves are by law permitted to be held, whether that transportation be by land, navigable river, or by the sea.

Article 5: That in addition to the provisions of the third paragraph of the second section of the fourth article of the Constitution of the United States, Congress shall have power to provide by law, and it shall be its duty so to provide, that the United States shall pay to the owner who shall apply for it, the full value of his fugitive slave in all cases where the marshall or other officer whose duty it was to arrest said fugitive was prevented from so doing by violence or intimidation, or when, after arrest, said fugitive was rescued by force, and the owner thereby prevented and obstructed in the pursuit of his remedy for the recovery of his fugitive slave under the said clause of the Constitution and the laws made in pursuance thereof. And in all such cases, when the United States shall pay for such fugitive, they shall have the right, in their own name, to sue the county in which said violence, intimidation, or rescue was committed, and to recover from it, with interest and damages, the amount paid by them for said fugitive slave. And the said county, after it has paid said

Delegates from the first seceding states met in Montgomery, Alabama, in February 1861 to draft a constitution for the Confederate government. They also named Jefferson Davis of Mississippi and Alexander Stephens of Georgia as president and vice-president, respectively. Neither man wanted the job, but in the first elections, held during November 1861, voters confirmed the convention's choices.

Jefferson Davis was inaugurated president of the Confederate States of America on February 18, 1861.

amount to the United States, may, for its indemnity, sue and recover from the wrong-doers or rescuers by whom the owner was prevented from the recovery of his fugitive slave, in like manner as the owner himslef might have sued and recovered.

Article 6: No future amendment of the Constitution shall affect the five preceding articles; nor the third paragraph of the second section of the first article of the Constitution; nor the third paragraph of the second section of the fourth article of said Constitution; and no amendment will be made to the Constitution which shall authorize or give to Congress any power to abolish or interfere with slavery in any of the States by whose laws it is, or may be, allowed or permitted.

And whereas, also, besides those causes of dissension embraced in the foregoing amendments proposed to the Constitution of the United States, there are others which come within the jurisdiction of Congress, and may be remedied by its legislative power; and whereas it is the desire of Congress, so far as its power will extend, to remove all just cause for the popular discontent and agitation which now disturb the peace of the country, and threaten the stability of its institutions; Therefore,

1. Resolved by the Senate and House of Representatives of the United States of America, in Congress assembled, That the laws now in force for the recovery of fugitive slaves are in strict pursuance of the plain and mandatory provisions of the Constitution, and have been sanctioned as valid and constitutional by the judgement of the Supreme Court of the United States.; that the slaveholding States are entitled to the faithful observance and execution of those laws, and that they ought not to be repealed, or so modified or changed as to impair their efficiency; and that laws ought to be made for the punishment of those who attempt by rescue of the slave, or other illegal means, to hinder or defeat the due execution of said laws.

2. That all State laws which conflict with the fugitive slave acts of Congress, or any other constitutional acts of Congress, or which, in their oper-

ation, impede, hinder, or delay the free course and due execution of any of said acts, are null and void by the plain provisions of the Constitution of the United States; yet those State laws, void as they are, have given color to practices, and led to consequences, which have obstructed the due administration and execution of acts of Congress, and especially the acts for the delivery of fugitive slaves, and have thereby contributed much to the discord and commotion now prevailing. Congress, therefore, in the present perilous juncture, does not deem it improper, respectfully and earnestly to recommend the repeal of those laws to the several States which have enacted them, or such legislative corections or explanations of them as may prevent their being used or perverted to such mischievous purposes.

3. That the act of the 18th of September, 1850, commonly called the fugitive slave law, ought to be so amended as to make the fee of the commissioner, mentioned in the eighth section of the act, equal in amount in the cases decided by him, whether his decision be in favor of or against the claimant. And to avoid misconstruction, the last clause of the fifth section of said act, which authorizes the person holding a warrent for the arrest or detention of a fugitive slave, to summon to his aid the posse comitatus, and which declares it to be the duty of all good citizens to assist him in its execution, ought to be so amended as to expressly limit the authority and duty to cases in which there shall be resistance or danger of resistance or rescue.

4. That the laws for the suppression of the African slave trade, and especially those prohibiting the importation of slaves in the United States, ought to be made effectual, and ought to be thoroughly executed; and all further enactments necessary to those ends ought to be promptly made.

Lincoln's First Inaugural Address

Lincoln left Springfield, Illinois, on February 11, 1861. As he moved toward Washington, D.C., he calmly explained to anxious crowds the necessity of preserving the Union. The journey became one continuous ovation. He reached Washington on February 23. Nine days later, before the stark, unfinished Capitol, Lincoln took his oath of office. In a masterly inaugural address, which had been carefully prepared, he invoked "the mystic chords of memory" in making a direct appeal to southerners. "In your hands, my dissatisfied fellow-countrymen, and not in mine, is the momentous issue of civil war. The government will not assail you. You can have no conflict without being yourselves the aggressors."

In compliance with a custom as old as the Government itself, I appear before you to address you briefly and to take in your presence the oath prescribed by the Constitution of the United States to be taken by the President "before he enters on the execution of this office."

I do not consider it necessary at present for me to discuss those matters of administration about which there is no special anxiety or excitement.

Apprehension seems to exist among the people of the Southern States that by the accession of a Republican Administration their property and their peace and personal security are to be endangered. There has never been any reasonable cause for such apprehension. Indeed, the most ample evidence to the contrary has all the while existed and been open to their inspection. It is found in nearly all the published speeches of him who now addresses you. I do but quote from one of those speeches when I declare that I have no purpose, directly or indirectly, to interfere with the institution of slavery in the States where it exists. I believe I have no lawful right to do so, and I have no inclination to do so.

Those who nominated and elected me did so with full knowledge that I had made this and many similar declarations and had never recanted them; and more than this, they placed in the platform for my acceptance, and as a law to themselves and to me, the clear and emphatic resolution which I now read:

> Resolved, That the maintenance inviolate of the rights of the States, and especially the right of each State to order and control its own domestic institutions according to its own judgment exclusively, is essential to that balance of power on which the perfection and endurance of our political fabric depend; and we denounce the lawless invasion by armed force of the soil of any State or Territory, no matter what pretext, as among the gravest of crimes.

I now reiterate these sentiments, and in doing so I only press upon the public attention the most conclusive evidence of which the case is susceptible that the property, peace, and security of no section are to be in any wise endangered by the now incoming Administration. I add, too, that all the protection which, consistently with the Constitution and the laws, can be given will be cheerfully given to all the States when lawfully demanded, for whatever cause—as cheerfully to one section as to another.

There is much controversy about the delivering up of fugitives from service or labor. The clause I now read is as plainly written in the Constitution as any other of its provisions:

> No person held to service or labor in one State, under the laws thereof, escaping into another, shall in consequence of any law or regulation therein be discharged from such service or labor, but shall be delivered up on claim of the party to whom such service or labor may be due.

It is scarcely questioned that this provision was intended by those who made it for the reclaiming of what we call fugitive slaves; and the intention of the lawgiver is the law. All members of Congress swear their support to the whole Constitution—to this provision as much as to any other. To the proposition, then, that slaves whose cases come within the terms of this clause "shall be delivered up" their oaths are unanimous. Now, if they would make the effort in good temper, could they not with nearly equal unanimity frame and pass a law by means of which to keep good that unanimous oath?

There is some difference of opinion whether this clause should be enforced by national or by State authority, but surely that difference is not a very material one. If the slave is to be surrendered, it can be of but little consequence to him or to others by which authority it is done. And should anyone in any case be content that his oath shall go unkept on a merely unsubstantial controversy as to how it shall be kept?

Again: In any law upon this subject ought not all the safeguards of liberty known in civilized and humane jurisprudence to be introduced, so that a free man be not in any case surrendered as a slave? And might it not be well at the same time to provide by law for the enforcement of that clause in the Constitution which guarantees that "the citizens of each State shall be entitled to all privileges and immunities of citizens in the several States"?

I take the official oath to-day with no mental reservations and with no purpose to construe the Constitution or laws by any hypercritical rules; and while I do not choose now to specify particular acts of Congress as proper to be enforced, I do suggest that it will be much safer for all, both in official and private stations, to conform to and abide by all those acts which stand unrepealed than to violate any of them trusting to find impunity in having them held to be unconstitutional.

It is seventy-two years since the first inauguration of a President under our National Constitution. During that period fifteen different and greatly distinguished citizens have in succession administered the executive branch of the Government. They have conducted it through many perils, and generally with great success. Yet, with all this scope of precedent, I now enter upon the same task for the brief constitutional term of four years under great and peculiar difficulty. A disruption of the Federal Union, heretofore only menaced, is now formidably attempted.

I hold that in contemplation of universal law and of the Constitution the Union of these States is perpetual. Perpetuity is implied, if not expressed, in the fundamental law of all national governments. It is safe to assert that no government proper ever had a provision in its organic law for its own termination. Continue to execute all the express provisions of our National Constitution, and the Union will endure forever, it being impossible to destroy it except by some action not provided for in the instrument itself.

Again: If the United States be not a government proper, but an association of States in the nature of contract merely, can it, as a contract, be peaceably unmade by less than all the parties who made it? One party to a contract may violate it— break it, so to speak—but does it not require all to lawfully rescind it?

Portrait of president-elect Lincoln from *Frank Leslie's Illustrated Newspaper.*

The 1860 presidential election is the most momentous in American history because the losing states refused to accept the results peacefully. The election was like the eye of a hurricane, a moment of dreadful calm with the foreboding sense of a greater storm to come.

Many myths now surround Lincoln—the tall, frugal, plainspoken man. Lincoln carefully assisted in cultivating stories about his humble origins. He was an excellent politician. However, few who voted for Lincoln at the 1860 Republican nominating convention realized that their greatest man had been nominated, a man who would become a towering humanitarian. To the majority of delegates, he simply appeared to have the best chance of winning.

Descending from these general principles, we find the proposition that in legal contemplation the Union is perpetual confirmed by the history of the Union itself. The Union is much older than the Constitution. It was formed, in fact, by the Articles of Association in 1774. It was matured and continued by the Declaration of Independence in 1776. It was further matured, and the faith of all the then thirteen States expressly plighted and engaged that it should be perpetual, by the Articles of Confederation in 1778. And finally, in 1787, one of the declared objects for ordaining and establishing the Constitution was "to form a more perfect Union."

But if destruction of the Union by one or by a part only of the States be lawfully possible, the Union is less perfect than before the Constitution, having lost the vital element of perpetuity.

It follows from these views that no State upon its own mere motion can lawfully get out of the Union; that resolves and ordinances to that effect are legally void, and that acts of violence within any State or States against the authority of the United States are insurrectionary or revolutionary, according to circumstances.

I therefore consider that in view of the Constitution and the laws the Union is unbroken, and to the extent of my ability, I shall take care, as the Constitution itself expressly enjoins upon me, that the laws of the Union be faithfully executed in all the States. Doing this I deem to be only a simple duty on my part, and I shall perform it so far as practicable unless my rightful masters, the American people, shall withhold the requisite means or in some authoritative manner direct the contrary. I trust this will not be regarded as a menace, but only as the declared purpose of the Union that it will constitutionally defend and maintain itself.

In doing this there needs to be no bloodshed or violence, and there shall be none unless it be forced upon the national authority. The power confided to me will be used to hold, occupy, and possess the property and places belonging to the Government and to collect the duties and imposts; but beyond what may be necessary for these objects, there will be no invasion, no using of force against or among the people anywhere. Where hostility to the United States in any interior locality shall be so great and universal as to prevent competent resident citizens from holding the Federal offices, there will be no attempt to force obnoxious strangers among the people for that object. While the strict legal right may exist in the Government to enforce the exercise of these offices, the attempt to do so would be so irritating and so nearly impracticable withal that I deem it better to forego for the time the uses of such offices.

The mails, unless repelled, will continue to be furnished in all parts of the Union. So far as possible the people everywhere shall have that sense of perfect security which is most favorable to calm thought and reflection. The course here indicated will be followed unless current events and experience shall show a modification or change to be proper, and in every case and exigency my best discretion will be exercised, according to circumstances actually existing and with a view and a hope of a peaceful solution of the national troubles and the restoration of fraternal sympathies and affections.

That there are persons in one section or another who seek to destroy the Union at all events and are glad of any pretext to do it I will neither affirm nor deny; but if there be such, I need address no word to them. To those, however, who really love the Union may I not speak?

Before entering upon so grave a matter as the destruction of our national fabric, with all its benefits, its memories, and its hopes, would it not be wise to ascertain precisely why we do it? Will you hazard so desperate a step while there is any possibility that any portion of the ills you fly from have no real existence? Will you, while the certain ills you fly to are greater than all the real ones you fly from, will you risk the commission of so fearful a mistake?

All profess to be content in the Union if all constitutional rights can be maintained. Is it true, then, that any right plainly written in the Constitution has been denied? I think not. Happily, the human mind is so constituted that no party can reach to the audacity of doing this. Think, if you can, of a single instance in which a plainly written provision of the Constitution has ever been denied. If by the mere force of numbers a majority should deprive a minority of any clearly written constitutional right, it might in a moral point of view justify revolution; certainly would if such right were a vital one. But such is not our case. All the vital rights of minorities and of individuals are so plainly assured to them by affirmations and negations, guaranties and prohibitions, in the Constitution that controversies never arise concerning them. But no organic law can ever be framed with a provision specifically applicable to every question which may occur in practical administration. No foresight can anticipate nor any document of reasonable length contain express provisions for all possible questions. Shall fugitives from labor be surrendered by national or by State authority? The Constitution does not expressly say. May Congress prohibit slavery in the Territories? The Constitution does not expressly say. Must Congress protect slavery in the Territories? The Constitution does not expressly say.

From questions of this class spring all our constitutional controversies, and we divide upon them into majorities and minorities. If the minority will not acquiesce, the majority must, or the Government must cease. There is no other alternative, for continuing the Government is acquiescence on one side or the other. If a minority in such case will secede rather than acquiesce, they make a precedent which in turn will divide and ruin them, for a minority of their own will secede from them whenever a majority refuses to be controlled by such minority. For instance, why may not any portion of a new confederacy a year or two hence arbitrarily secede again, precisely as portions of the present Union now claim to secede from it? All who cherish disunion sentiments are now being educated to the exact temper of doing this.

Is there such perfect identity of interests among the States to compose a new union as to produce harmony only and prevent renewed secession?

Plainly the central idea of secession is the essence of anarchy. A majority held in restraint by constitutional checks and limitations, and always changing easily with deliberate changes of popular opinions and sentiments, is the only true sovereign of a free people. Whoever rejects it does of necessity fly to anarchy or to despotism. Unanimity is impossible. The rule of a minority, as a permanent arrangement, is wholly inadmissible; so that, rejecting the majority principle, anarchy or despotism in some form is all that is left.

I do not forget the position assumed by some that constitutional questions are to be decided by the Supreme Court, nor do I deny that such decisions must be binding in any case upon the parties to a suit as to the object of that suit, while they are also entitled to very high respect and consideration in all parallel cases by all other departments of the Government. And while it is obviously possible that such decision may be erroneous in any given case, still the evil effect following it, being limited to that particular case, with the chance that it may be overruled and never become a precedent for other cases, can better be borne than could the evils of a different practice. At the same time, the candid citizen must confess that if the policy of the Government upon vital questions affecting the whole people is to be irrevocably fixed by decisions of the Supreme Court, the instant they are made in ordinary litigation between parties in personal actions the people will have ceased to be their own rulers, having to that extent practically resigned their Government into the hands of that eminent tribunal. Nor is there in this view any assault upon the court or the judges. It is a duty from which they may not shrink to decide cases properly brought before them, and it is no fault of theirs if others seek to turn their decisions to political purposes.

One section of our country believes slavery is right and ought to be extended, while the other believes it is wrong and ought not to be extended. This is the only substantial dispute. The fugitive-slave clause of the Constitution and the law for the suppression of the foreign slave trade are each as well enforced, perhaps, as any law can ever be in a community where the moral sense of the people imperfectly supports the law itself. The great body of the people abide by the dry legal obligation in both cases, and a few break over in each. This, I think, can not be perfectly cured, and it would be worse in both cases after the separation of the sections than before. The foreign slave trade, now imperfectly suppressed, would be ultimately revived without restriction in one section, while fugitive slaves, now only partially surrendered, would not be surrendered at all by the other.

Physically speaking, we can not separate. We can not remove our respective sections from each other nor build an impassable wall between them. A husband and wife may be divorced and go out of the presence and beyond the reach of each other, but the different parts of our country can not do this. They can not but remain face to face, and intercourse, either amicable or hostile, must continue between them. Is it possible, then, to make that intercourse more advantageous or more satisfactory after separation than before? Can aliens make treaties easier than friends can make laws? Can treaties be more faithfully enforced between aliens than laws can among friends? Suppose you go to war, you can not fight always; and when, after much loss on both sides and no gain on either, you cease fighting, the identical old questions, as to terms of intercourse, are again upon you.

This country, with its institutions, belongs to the people who inhabit it. Whenever they shall grow weary of the existing Government, they can exercise their constitutional right of amending it or their revolutionary right to dismember or overthrow it. I can not be ignorant of the fact that many worthy and patriotic citizens are desirous of having the National Constitution amended. While I make no recommendation of amendments, I fully recognize the rightful authority of the people over the whole subject, to be exercised in either of the modes prescribed in the instrument itself; and I should, under existing circumstances, favor rather than oppose a fair opportunity being afforded the people to act upon it. I will venture to add that to me the convention mode seems preferable, in that it allows amendments to originate with the people themselves, instead of only permitting them to take or reject propositions originated by others, not especially chosen for the purpose, and which might not be precisely such as they would wish to either accept or refuse. I understand a proposed amendment to the Constitution—which amendment, however, I have not seen—has passed Congress, to the effect that the Federal Government shall never interfere with the domestic institutions of the States, including that of persons held to service. To avoid misconstruction of what I have said, I depart from my purpose not to speak of particular amendments so far as to say that, holding such a provision to now be implied constitutional law, I have no objection to its being made express and irrevocable.

The Chief Magistrate derives all his authority from the people, and they have referred none upon him to fix terms for the separation of the States. The people themselves can do this if also they choose, but the Executive as such has nothing to do with it. His duty is to administer the present Government as it came to his hands and to transmit it unimpaired by him to his successor.

Why should there not be a patient confidence in the ultimate justice of the people? Is there any better or equal hope in the world? In our present differences, is either party without faith of being in the right? If the Almighty Ruler of Nations, with His eternal truth and justice, be on your side of the North, or on yours of the South, that truth and that justice will surely prevail by the judgment of this great tribunal of the American people.

By the frame of the Government under which we live this same people have wisely given their public servants but little power for mischief, and have with equal wisdom provided for the return of that little to their own hands at very short intervals. While the people retain their virtue and vigilance no Administration by any extreme of wickedness or folly can very seriously injure the Government in the short space of four years.

My countrymen, one and all, think calmly and well upon this whole subject. Nothing valuable can be lost by taking time. If there be an object to hurry any of you in hot haste to a step which you would never take deliberately, that object will be frustrated by taking time; but no good object can be frustrated by it. Such of you as are now dissatisfied still have the old Constitution unim-paired, and, on the sensitive point, the laws of your own framing under it; while the new Administration will have no immediate power, if it would, to change either. If it were admitted that you who are dissatisfied hold the right side in the dispute, there still is no single good reason for precipitate action. Intelligence, patriotism, Christianity, and a firm reliance on Him who has never yet forsaken this favored land are still competent to adjust in the best way all our present difficulty.

In your hands, my dissatisfied fellow-countrymen, and not in mine, is the momentous issue of civil war. The Government will not assail you. You can have no conflict without being yourselves the aggressors. You have no oath registered in heaven to destroy the Government, while I shall have the most solemn one to "preserve, protect, and defend it."

I am loath to close. We are not enemies, but friends. We must not be enemies. Though passion may have strained it must not break our bonds of affection. The mystic chords of memory, stretching from every battlefield and patriot grave to every living heart and hearthstone all over this broad land, will yet swell the chorus of the Union, when again touched, as surely they will be, by the better angels of our nature.

Message to Congress, July 4, 1861

The Civil War began on April 12, 1861, with the firing on Fort Sumter in Charleston harbor by South Carolinians. On April 15, Lincoln declared that "an insurrection" existed and he called for 75,000 three-month volunteers to put down combinations "too powerful to be suppressed by the ordinary course of judicial proceedings." At the same time he called Congress to meet in special session on July 4, 1861.

In this masterly message to Congress, Lincoln explained his policies since the firing on Fort Sumter. He recounted the steps that had led to war, stated his concept on the significance of the Union, and appealed for ratification of his acts as well as for future cooperation.

Having been convened on an extraordinary occasion, as authorized by the Constitution, your attention is not called to any ordinary subject of legislation.

At the beginning of the present Presidential term, four months ago, the functions of the Federal Government were found to be generally suspended within the several States of South Carolina, Georgia, Alabama, Mississippi, Louisiana, and Florida, excepting only those of the Post-office Department.

Within these States, all the forts, arsenals, dockyards, custom-houses, and the like, including the movable and stationary property in and about them, had been seized, and were held in open hostility to this government, excepting only Forts Pickens, Taylor, and Jefferson, on and near the Florida coast, and Fort Sumter, in Charleston Harbor, South Carolina. The forts thus seized had been put in improved condition; new ones had been built; and armed forces had been organized, and were organizing, all avowedly with the same hostile purpose.

The forts remaining in the possession of the Federal government in and near these States were either besieged or menaced by warlike preparations, and especially Fort Sumter was nearly surrounded by well-protected hostile batteries, with guns equal in quality to the best of its own, and outnumbering the latter as perhaps ten to one. A disproportion-ate share, of the Federal muskets and rifles had somehow found their way into these States, and had been seized to be used against the government. Accumulations of the public revenue lying within them had been seized for the same object. The navy was scattered in distant seas, leaving but a very small part of it within the immediate reach of the government. Officers of the Federal army and navy, had resigned in great numbers; and of those resigning a large proportion had taken up arms against the government. Simultaneously, and in connection with all this, the purpose to sever the Federal Union, was openly avowed. In accordance with this purpose, an ordinance had been adopted in each of these States, declaring the States respectively to be separated from the National Union. A formula for instituting a combined government of these states had been promulgated; and this illegal organization, in the character of confederate States was already invoking recognition, aid, and intervention, from foreign powers.

Finding this condition of things, and believing it to be an imperative duty upon the incoming executive, to prevent, if possible, the consummation of such attempt to destroy the Federal Union, a choice of means to that end became indispensable. This choice was made and was declared in the inaugural address. The policy chosen looked to the exhaustion of all peaceful measures, before a resort to any stronger ones. It sought only to hold the public places and property not already wrested from the government, and to collect the revenue, relying for the rest on time, discussion, and the ballot-box. It promised a continuance of the mails, at government expense, to the very people who were resisting the government; and it gave repeated pledges against any disturbance to any of the people, or any of their rights. Of all that which a president might constitutionally and justifiably do in such a case, everything was foreborne, without which, it was believed possible to keep the government on foot. [. . .]

It was believed, however, that to so abandon [Fort Sumter] under the circumstances, would be utterly ruinous; that the necessity under which it was to be done, would not be fully understood; that, by many, it would be construed as a part of a voluntary policy; that, at home, it would discourage the friends of the Union, embolden its adversaries, and go far to insure to the latter a recognition abroad; that in fact it would be our national destruction consummated. This could not be allowed. Starvation was not yet upon the garrison; and ere it would be reached, Fort Pickens might be reinforced. This last, would be a clear indication of policy, and would better enable the country to accept the evacuation of Fort Sumter, as a military necessity. An order was at once directed to be sent for the landing of the troops from the Steamship *Brooklyn* into Fort Pickens. This order could not go by land, but must take the longer and slower route by sea. The first return news from the order was received just one week before the fall of Fort Sumter. The news itself was, that the officer commanding the *Sabine*, to which vessel the troops had been transferred from the *Brooklyn*, acting upon some *quasi* armistice of the late administration (and of the existence of which, the present administration, up to the time the order was dispatched, had only too vague and uncertain rumors, to fix attention) had refused to land the troops. To now re-inforce Fort Pickens, before a crisis would be reached at Fort Sumter was impossible—rendered so by the near exhaustion of provisions in the latter-named fort. In precaution against such a conjuncture, the government had, a few days before, commenced preparing an expedition, as well adapted as might be to relieve Fort Sumter, which expedition was intended to be ultimately used, or not, according to circumstances. The strongest anticipated case for using it was now presented, and it was resolved to send it forward. As had been intended in this contingency, it was also resolved to notify the governor of South Carolina that he might expect an attempt would be made to provision the fort; and that, if the attempt should not be resisted, there would be no effort to throw in men, arms, or ammunition, without further notice, or in case of an attack upon the fort. This notice was accordingly given; whereupon the fort was attacked and bombarded to its fall, without even awaiting the arrival of the provisioning expedition.

It is thus seen that the assault upon and reduction of Fort Sumter was in no sense a matter of self defence on the part of the assailants. They well knew that the garrison in the Fort could, by no possibility, commit aggression upon them. They knew—they were expressly notified—that the giving of bread to the few brave and hungry men of the garrison was all which would on that occasion be attempted, unless themselves, by resisting so much, should provoke more. They knew that this Government desired to keep the garrison in the Fort, not to assail them, but merely to maintain visible possession, and thus to preserve the Union from actual, and immediate dissolution—trusting, as hereinbefore stated, to time, discussion, and the ballot-box for final adjustment; and they assailed and reduced the Fort for precisely the reverse object— to drive out the visible authority of the Federal Union, and thus force it to immediate dissolution. [. . .]

Unquestionably the States have the powers and rights reserved to them in and by the National Constitution; but among these surely are not included all conceivable powers, however mischievous or destructive, but, at most, such only as were known in the world at the time as governmental powers; and certainly a power to destroy the government itself had never been known as a governmental, as a merely administrative power. This relative matter of national power, and State rights, as a principle, is no other than the principle of generality and locality. Whatever concerns the whole should be confided to the whole—to the General Government; while whatever concerns only the State should be left exclusively to the State. This is all there is of original principle about it. Whether the National Constitution in defining boundaries between the two has applied the principle with exact accuracy, is not to be questioned. We are all bound by that defining, without question.

What is now combatted is the position that secession is consistent with the Constitution—is lawful, and peaceful. It is not contended that there is any express law for it; and nothing should ever be implied as law which leads to unjust or absurd consequences. The nation purchased with money the countries out of which several of these States were formed. Is it just that they shall go off without leave and without refunding? The nation paid very large sums (in the aggregate, I believe, nearly a hundred millions) to relieve Florida of the aboriginal tribes. Is it just that she shall now be off without consent or without making any return? The nation is now in debt for money applied to the benefit of these so-called seceding States in common with the rest. Is it just either that creditors shall go unpaid or the remaining States pay the whole? A part of the present national debt was contracted to pay the old debts of Texas. Is it just that she shall leave and pay no part of this herself?

Again, if one State may secede, so may another; and when all shall have seceded, none is left to pay the debts. Is this quite just to creditors? Did we notify them of this sage view of ours, when we borrowed their money?

If we now recognize this doctrine by allowing the seceders to go in peace, it is difficult to see what we can do if others choose to go or to extort terms upon which they will promise to remain.

The seceders insist that our Constitution admits of secession. They have assumed to make a national constitution of their own, in which of necessity they have either discarded or retained the right of secession as they insist it exists in ours. If they have discarded it, they thereby admit that on principle it ought not to be in ours. If they have retained it by their own construction of ours they show that to be consistent they must secede from one another whenever they shall find it the easiest way of settling their debts, or effecting any

Foldout brass book-locket with photographs of Lincoln and Union generals.
The number of American soldiers killed during the Civil War was considerably higher than in any other war in which the United States has taken part. More than 618,000 men were killed (North: 360,000; South: 258,000). During World War II (1941–45), battlefield casualties for the United States were 407,000. The total U.S. population in 1940 was nearly 132 million, compared to 31.4 million in 1860.

other selfish or unjust object. The principle itself is one of disintegration, and upon which no government can possibly endure.

If all the States save one should assert the power to drive that one out of the Union, it is presumed the whole class of seceder politicians would at once deny the power and denounce the act as the greatest outrage upon State rights. But suppose that precisely the same act, instead of being called "driving the one out," should be called "the seceding of the others from that one," it would be exactly what the seceders claim to do; unless, indeed, they make the point that the one, because it is a minority, may rightfully do what the others, because they are a majority, may not rightfully do. These politicians are subtle and profound on the rights of minorities. They are not partial to that power which made the Constitution, and speaks from the preamble, calling itself "We, the People."

It may well be questioned whether there is today a majority of the legally qualified voters of any State, except perhaps South Carolina, in favor of dis-union. There is much reason to believe that the Union men are the majority in many, if not in every other one, of the so-called seceded States. The contrary has not been demonstrated in any one of them. It is ventured to affirm this, even of Virginia and Tennessee; for the result of an election held in military camps, where the bayonets are all on one side of the question voted upon, can scarcely be considered as demonstrating popular sentiment. At such an election, all that large class who are at once for the Union and against coercion, would be coerced to vote against the Union. It may be affirmed, without extravagance, that the free institutions we enjoy have developed the powers and improved the condition of our whole people beyond any example in the world. Of this we now have a striking and an impressive illustration. So large an army as the government has now on foot was never before known without a soldier in it but who had taken his place there of his own free choice. But more than this: there are many single regiments whose members, one and another, possess full practical knowledge of all the arts, sciences, professions, and whatever else, whether useful or elegant, is known in the world; and there is scarcely one from which there could not be selected a president, a cabinet, a congress, and perhaps a court, abundantly competent to administer the government itself. Nor do I say this is not true also in the army of our late friends, now adversaries, in this contest; but if it is, so much better the reason why the government, which has conferred such benefits on both them and us, should not be broken up. Whoever in any section proposes to abandon such a government would do well to consider in deference to what principle it is that he does it—what better he is likely to get in its stead—whether the substitute will give, or be intended to give, so much of good to the people. There are some foreshadowings on this subject. Our adversaries have adopted some Declarations of Independence; in which, unlike the good old one, penned by Jefferson, they omit the words "all men are created equal." Why? They have adopted a temporary national constitution, in the preamble of which, unlike our good old one, signed by Washington, they omit "We, the People," and substitute "We, the deputies of the sovereign and independent States." Why? Why this deliberate pressing out of view, the rights of men, and the authority of the people?

This is essentially a People's contest. On the side of the Union, it is a struggle for maintaining in the world that form and substance of government whose leading object is to elevate the condition of men—to lift artificial weights from all shoulders; to clear the paths of laudable pursuit for all; to afford all an unfettered start, and a fair chance, in the race of life. Yielding to partial and temporary departures, from necessity, this is the leading object of the government for whose existence we contend. [. . .]

It was with the deepest regret that the Executive found the duty of employing the war-power, in defence of the government, forced upon him. He could but perform this duty, or surrender the existence of the government. No compromise, by public servants, could, in this case, be a cure; not that compromises are not often proper, but that no popular government can long

Ferrotype portraits, 1-1/2" in size, set in ornamental brass frames. Abraham Lincoln and Hannibal Hamlin, top row, Jefferson Davis and Alexander Stephens, below.

survive a marked precedent, that those who carry an election, can only save the government from immediate destruction, by giving up the main point, upon which the people gave the election. The people themselves, and not their servants, can safely reverse their own deliberate decisions. As a private citizen, the Executive could not have consented that these institutions shall perish; much less could he, in betrayal of so vast, and so sacred a trust, as these free people had confided to him. He felt that he had no moral right to shrink; nor even to count the chances of his own life, in what might follow. In full view of his great responsibility, he has, so far, done what he has deemed his duty. You will now, according to your own judgment, perform yours. He sincerely hopes that your views, and your action, may so accord with his, as to assure all faithful citizens, who have been disturbed in their rights, of a certain, and speedy restoration to them, under the Constitution, and the laws. And having thus chosen our course, without guile, and with pure purpose, let us renew our trust in God, and go forward without fear, and with manly hearts.

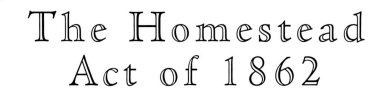

The Homestead Act of 1862

Congress passed the Homestead Act in 1862 after half a century of legislative efforts by Western farmers. (A homestead is the home and land occupied by a family.) The act, although not entirely successful, offered any citizen, or person intending to become a citizen, who was the head of a family and over 21 years of age, 160 acres of the surveyed public domain free after five years of continued residence and the payment of a registration fee.

HE FIRST DIVISION—NO. 1. WAGON WITH INSCRIPTIONS OF YOUNG MENS INDEPENDENT
UCK BEARING INSCRIPTION AND SHIELDS OF THE THIRTEEN STATES.—SEE PAGE ONE

BE IT ENACTED by the Senate and House of Representatives of the United States of America in Congress assembled, That any person who is the head of a family, or who has arrived at the age of twenty-one years, and is a citizen of the United States, or who shall have filed his declaration of intention to become such, as required by the naturalization laws of the United States, and who has never borne arms against the United States Government or given aid and comfort to its enemies, shall, from and after the first of January, eighteen hundred and sixty-three, be entitled to enter one quarter section or a less quantity of unappropriated public lands, upon which said person may have filed a preemption claim, or which may, at the time the application is made, be subject to preemption at one dollar and twenty-five cents, or less, per acre; or eighty acres or less of such unappropriated lands, at two dollars and fifty cents per acre, to be located in a body, in conformity to the legal subdivisions of the public lands, and after the same shall have been surveyed: Provided, That any person owning and residing on land may, under the provisions of this act, enter other land lying contiguous to his or her said land, which shall not, with the land so already owned and occupied, exceed in the aggregate, one hundred and sixty acres.

Section 2. And be it further enacted, That the person applying for the benefit of this act shall, upon application to the register of the land office in which he or she is about to make such entry, make affidavit before the said register or receiver that he or she is the head of a family, or is twenty-one years or more of age, or shall have performed service in the army or navy of the United States, and that he has never borne arms against the Government of the United States or given aid and comfort to its enemies, and that such application is made for his or her exclusive use and benefit, and that said entry is made for the purpose of actual settlement and cultivation, and not either directly or indirectly for the use or benefit of any other person or persons whomsoever; and upon filing the said affidavit with the register or receiver, and on payment of ten dollars, he or she shall thereupon be permitted to enter the quantity of land specified: Provided, however, That no certificate shall be given or patent issued therefor until the expiration of five years from the date of such entry; and if, at the expiration of such time, or at any time within two years thereafter, the person making such entry; or, if he be dead, his widow; or in case of her death, his heirs or devisee; or in the case of a widow making such entry, her heirs or devisee, in the case of her death; shall prove by two credible witnesses that he, she, or they have resided upon or cultivated the same for the term of five years immediately succeeding the time of filing the affidavit aforesaid, and shall make affidavit that no part of said land has been alienated, and he has borne true allegiance to the Government of the United States; then, in such case, he, she, or they, if at that time a citizen of the United States, shall be entitled to a patent, as in other cases provided for by law: And, provided, further, That in case of the death of both father and mother, leaving an infant child, or children, under twenty-one years of age, the right and fee shall enure to the benefit of said infant child or children; and the executor, administrator, or guardian may, at any time within two years after the death of the surviving parent, and in accordance with the laws of the State in which such children for the time being have their domicil, sell said land for the benefit of said infants, but for no other purpose; and the purchaser shall acquire the absolute title by the purchase, and be entitled to a patent from the United States, on payment of the office fees and sum of money herein specified.

Section 3. And be it further enacted, That the register of the land office shall note all such applications on the tract books and plats of his office, and keep a register of all such entries, and make return thereof to the General Land Office, together with the proof upon which they have been founded.

Section 4. And be it further enacted, That no lands acquired under the provisions of this act shall in any event become liable to the satisfaction of any debt or debts contracted prior to the issuing of the patent therefor.

Section 5. And be it further enacted, That if, at any time after the filing of the affidavit, as required in the second section of this act, and before the expiration of the five years aforesaid, it shall be proven, after due notice to the settler, to the satisfaction of the register of the land office, that the person having filed such affidavit shall have actually changed his or her residence, or abandoned the said land for more than six months at any time, then and in that event the land so entered shall revert to the government.

Section 6. And be it further enacted, That no individual shall be permitted to acquire title to more than one quarter section under the provisions of this act; and that the Commissioner of the General Land Office is hereby required to prepare and issue such rules and regulations, consistent with

Silk ribbon from photographic portrait by Matthew Brady taken on February 27, 1860, hours before Lincoln delivered his Cooper Union speech in New York City.

this act, as shall be necessary and proper to carry its provisions into effect; and that the registers and receivers of the several land offices shall be entitled to receive the same compensation for any lands entered under the provisions of this act that they are now entitled to receive when the same quantity of land is entered with money, one half to be paid by the person making the

Lincoln shaving mug, circa 1862.

The Homestead Act of 1862 required that the owner must live on and work the land for five years. This was to make sure that the land went to actual settlers. As an alternative, land covered by this act could be acquired after six months residence at $1.25 an acre—about the daily wage of a laborer. Such homesteads were to be exempt from attachment for debt. However, by dishonest use of the law, speculators, instead of actual settlers, often obtained large tracts of land. For example, speculators falsely met the provisions of the law by putting down a few logs as the foundation of a cabin and scattering some seed. Still, the act did encourage settlement of the West.

application at the time of so doing, and the other half on the issue of the certificate by the person to whom it may be issued; but this shall not be construed to enlarge the maximum of compensation now prescribed by law for any register or receiver: Provided, That nothing contained in this act shall be so construed as to impair or interfere in any manner whatever with existing preemption rights: And provided, further, That all persons who may have filed their applications for a preemption right prior to the passage of this act, shall be entitled to all privileges of this act: Provided, further, That no person who has served or may hereafter serve, for period of not less than fourteen days in the army or navy of the United States, either regular or volunteer, under the laws thereof, during the existence of an actual war, domestic or foreign, shall be deprived of the benefits of this act of account of not having attained the age of twenty-one years.

Section 7. And be it further enacted, That the fifth section of the act entitled "An act in addition to an act more effectually to provide for the punishment of certain crimes against the United States, and for other purposes," approved the third of March, in the year eighteen hundred and fifty-seven, shall extend to all oaths, affirmations, and affidavits, required or authorized by this act.

Discussions about secession had been earnestly carried on for many years. Hardly any aspect of the subject had been untouched. However, the actual causes of secession in 1860–61 were plainly expressed by southern conventions, which repealed their state resolutions originally ratifying the Constitution. "The people of the Northern states," declared Mississippi, "have assumed a revolutionary position toward the Southern states." The Mississippi convention also wrote:

- "They have enticed our slaves from us, and obstructed their return."
- The northern states illegally claim the right "to exclude slavery from the territories, and from any state henceforth admitted to the Union."
- They have "insulted and outraged our citizens when travelling among them. . . . by taking their servants and liberating the same."

To these claims South Carolina added:

- "They [the northern states] have denounced as sinful the institution of slavery; they have permitted the open establishment among them of [abolitionist] societies."
- "They have encouraged and assisted thousands of our slaves to leave their homes; and those who remain, have been incited by emissaries, books, and pictures to servile insurrection."
- They "have united in the election of a man to the high office of the President of the United States whose opinions and purposes are hostile to slavery.

Section 8. And be it further enacted, That nothing in this act shall be so construed as to prevent any person who has availed him or herself of the benefits of the first section of this act, from paying the minimum price, or the price to which the same may have graduated, for the quantity of land so entered at any time before the expiration of the five years, and obtaining a patent therefor from the government, as in other cases provided by law, on making proof of settlement and cultivation as provided by existing laws granting preemption rights.

The Pacific Railway Act

On July 1, 1862, Lincoln signed this act, which authorized construction of a transcontinental railroad. Railroad companies received land grants as an incentive to build a railroad which would link the west and east coasts. A second bill, passed in 1864, further increased both land and financial grants to railroad companies. Altogether, more than 45 million acres of land were granted to the Union Pacific and Central Pacific, and more than $60 million loaned to build the railroad. The transcontinental railroad was completed on May 10, 1869.

An Act to aid in the Construction of a Railroad and Telegraph Line from the Missouri River to the Pacific Ocean. [. . .]

Be it enacted, That [names of corporators]; together with five commissioners to be appointed by the Secretary of the Interior [. . .] are hereby created and erected into a body corporate [. . .] by the name [. . .] of "The Union Pacific Railroad Company" [. . .] ; and the said corporation is hereby authorized and empowered to lay out, locate, construct, furnish, maintain and enjoy a continuous railroad and telegraph [. . .] from a point on the one hundredth meridian of longitude west from Greenwich, between the south margin of the valley of the Republican River and the north margin of the valley of the Platte River, to the western boundary of Nevada Territory, upon the route and terms hereinafter provided [. . .]

Sec. 2. That the right of way through the public lands be [. . .] granted to said company for the construction of said railroad and telegraph line; and the right [. . .] is hereby given to said company to take from the public lands adjacent to the line of said road, earth, stone, timber, and other materials for the construction thereof; said right of way is granted to said railroad to the extent of two hundred feet in width on each side of said railroad when it may pass over the public lands, including all necessary grounds, for stations, buildings, workshops, and depots, machine shops, switches, side tracks, turn tables, and water stations. The United States shall extinguish as rapidly as may be the Indian titles to all lands falling under the operation of this act [. . .]

Sec. 3. That there be [. . .] granted to the said company, for the purpose of aiding in the construction of said railroad and telegraph line, and to secure the safe and speedy transportation of mails, troops, munitions of war, and public stores thereon, every alternate section of public land, designated by odd numbers, to the amount of five alternate sections per mile on each side of said railroad, on the line thereof, and within the limits of ten miles on each side of said road [. . .] Provided That all mineral lands shall be excepted from the operation of this act; but where the same shall contain timber, the timber thereon is hereby granted to said company [. . .]

Sec. 5. That for the purposes herein mentioned the Secretary of the Treasury shall [. . .] in accordance with the provisions of this act, issue to said company bonds of the United States of one thousand dollars each, payable in thirty years after date, paying six per centum per annum interest [. . .] to the amount of sixteen of said bonds per mile for each section of forty miles; and to secure the repayment to the United States [. . .] of the amount of said bonds [. . .] the issue of said bonds [. . .] shall ipso facto constitute a first mortgage on the whole line of the railroad and telegraph [. . .]

Jefferson Davis (1808–1889), pictured in this ferrotype medallion, had held several military and political positions before accepting the presidency of the Confederate States of America. However, the idea of the South as a social and economic unit, a nation within the Union, was a constant in his mind. For example, while Franklin Pierce's Secretary of War (1853–57), Davis eagerly lobbied for expansion southward toward Mexico and Latin America. He promoted a grand scheme for a transcontinental railroad that would be close to the Mexican border and terminate in that part of southern California which Southerners had attempted to obtain in 1850. To make such a railroad possible, Davis convinced President Pierce and Secretary of State William Marcy to acquire from Mexico the region now known as the Gadsden Purchase (1853). To demonstrate the practicability of such a railroad, he sent an expedition of engineers, artists, and scientists who prepared a monumental report on the Southwest, which the government published in ten large volumes.

Sec. 9. That the Leavenworth, Pawnee and Western Railroad Company of Kansas are hereby authorized to construct a railroad and telegraph line [. . .] upon the same terms and conditions in all respects as are provided [for construction of the Union Pacific Railroad] The Central Pacific Railroad Company of California are hereby authorized to construct a railroad and telegraph line from the Pacific coast [. . .] to the eastern boundaries of California, upon the same terms and conditions in all respects [as are provided for the Union Pacific Railroad].

Sec. 10 [. . .] And the Central Pacific Railroad Company of California after completing its road across said State, is authorized to continue the construction of said railroad and telegraph through the Territories of the United States to the Missouri River [. . .] upon the terms and conditions provided in this act in relation to the Union Pacific Railroad Company, until said roads shall meet and connect [. . .]

Sec. 11. That for three hundred miles of said road most mountainous and difficult of construction, to wit: one hundred and fifty miles westerly from the eastern base of the Rocky Mountains, and one hundred and fifty miles eastwardly from the western base of the Sierra Nevada mountains [. . .] the bonds to be issued to aid in the construction thereof shall be treble the number per mile hereinbefore provided [. . .] and between the sections last named of one hundred and fifty miles each, the bonds to be issued to aid in the construction thereof shall be double the number per mile first mentioned [. . .]

Letter to Horace Greeley

Horace Greeley, the influential editor of the *New York Tribune*, was an implacable foe of slavery. His impatience with Lincoln's vacillating policy culminated in a signed emancipation editorial, "The Prayer of Twenty Millions" (August 19, 1862). Three days later, Lincoln responded with an open letter to Greeley—that is, a letter meant for widespread public attention. Lincoln reiterated that preservation of the Union remained the purpose of the war but he hinted that partial or even total emancipation might become necessary to accomplish that purpose.

I have just read yours of the nineteenth addressed to myself through the *New-York Tribune*. If there be in it any statements, or assumptions of fact, which I may know to be erroneous, I do not, now and here, controvert them. If there be in it any inferences which I may believe to be falsely drawn, I do not now and here, argue against them. If there be perceptable in it an impatient and dictatorial tone, I waive it in deference to an old friend, whose heart I have always supposed to be right.

As to the policy I "seem to be pursuing" as you say, I have not meant to leave any one in doubt.

I would save the Union. I would save it the shortest way under the Constitution. The sooner the national authority can be restored; the nearer the Union will be "the Union as it was." If there be those who would not save the Union, unless they could at the same time save slavery, I do not agree with them. If there be those who would not save the Union unless they could at the same time destroy slavery, I do not agree with them. My paramount object in this struggle is to save the Union, and is not either to save or to destroy slavery. If I could save the Union without freeing any slave I would do it, and if I could save it by freeing all the slaves I would do it; and if I could save it by freeing some and leaving others alone I would also do that. What I do about slavery, and the colored race, I do because I believe it helps to save the Union; and what I forbear, I forbear because I do not believe it would help to save the Union. I shall do less whenever I shall believe what I am doing hurts the cause, and I shall do more whenever I shall believe doing more will help the cause. I shall try to correct errors when shown to be errors; and I shall adopt new views so fast as they shall appear to be true views.

I have here stated my purpose according to my view of official duty; and I intend no modification of my oft-expressed personal wish that all men everywhere could be free.

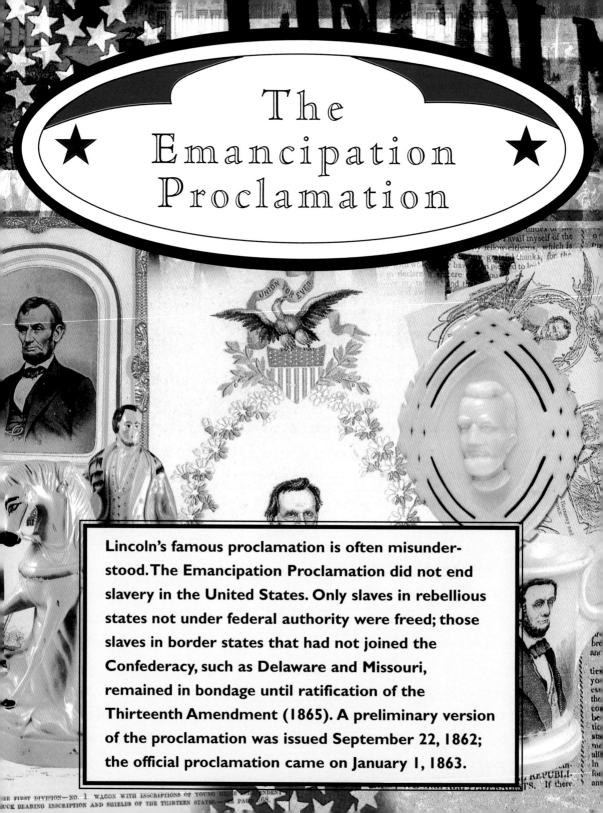

The Emancipation Proclamation

Lincoln's famous proclamation is often misunderstood. The Emancipation Proclamation did not end slavery in the United States. Only slaves in rebellious states not under federal authority were freed; those slaves in border states that had not joined the Confederacy, such as Delaware and Missouri, remained in bondage until ratification of the Thirteenth Amendment (1865). A preliminary version of the proclamation was issued September 22, 1862; the official proclamation came on January 1, 1863.

WHEREAS on the 22nd day of September, A.D. 1862, a proclamation was issued by the President of the United States, containing, among other things, the following, to wit:

"That on the 1st day of January, A.D. 1863, all persons held as slaves within any State or designated part of a State the people whereof shall then be in rebellion against the United States shall be then, thenceforward, and forever free; and the executive government of the United States, including the military and naval authority thereof, will recognize and maintain the freedom of such persons and will do no act or acts to repress such persons, or any of them, in any efforts they may make for their actual freedom.

"That the executive will on the 1st day of January aforesaid, by proclamation, designate the States and parts of States, if any, in which the people thereof, respectively, shall then be in rebellion against the United States; and the fact that any State or the people thereof shall on that day be in good faith represented in the Congress of the United States by members chosen thereto at elections wherein a majority of the qualified voters of such States shall have participated shall, in the absence of strong countervailing testimony, be deemed conclusive evidence that such State and the people thereof are not then in rebellion against the United States."

Now, therefore, I, Abraham Lincoln, President of the United States, by virtue of the power in me vested as Commander-In-Chief of the Army and Navy of the United States in time of actual armed rebellion against the authority and government of the United States, and as a fit and necessary war measure for suppressing said rebellion, do, on this 1st day of January, A.D. 1863, and in accordance with my purpose so to do, publicly proclaimed for the full period of one hundred days from the first day above mentioned, order and designate as the States and parts of States wherein the people thereof, respectively, are this day in rebellion against the United

A. Lincoln.   Mrs. A. Lincoln.

Tintype portraits of Lincoln and his wife Mary. During the presidency of her husband, Mary Todd Lincoln (1818–1882) focused on social affairs. Born in the South, she was subjected to criticism, much of which was gossip and malicious slander. Even the touches of White House social gaiety, with which she relieved the strain of wartime anxiety, were criticized as inappropriate. Contemporary writers describe Mrs. Lincoln as a short, plump brunette with a "certain formal beauty." Her critics claim she had an "irritable temper" and accused her of interfering in political decisions.

States the following, to wit:

> Arkansas, Texas, Louisiana (except the parishes of St. Bernard, Palquemines, Jefferson, St. John, St. Charles, St. James, Ascension, Assumption, Terrebone, Lafourche, St. Mary, St. Martin, and Orleans, including the city of New Orleans), Mississippi, Alabama, Florida, Georgia, South Carolina, North Carolina, and Virginia (except the forty-eight counties designated as West Virginia, and also the counties of Berkeley, Accomac, Northhampton, Elizabeth City, York, Princess Anne, and Norfolk, including the cities of Norfolk and Portsmouth), and which excepted parts are for the present left precisely as if this proclamation were not issued.

And by virtue of the power and for the purpose aforesaid, I do order and

From the day he took office, Lincoln "struggled," as he said, with the issue of freeing the slaves without compensating their owners. Every kind of pressure—religious, political, and personal—was brought on him to make such a declaration. However, Lincoln's policy dealing with slavery was a matter of slow development.

Lincoln finally reached his decision during the summer of 1862—and on September 22, he declared that "persons held as slaves" within areas "in rebellion against the United States" would be free on January 1, 1863.

The Emancipation Proclamation was far from an abolition document as it did not apply to Tennessee, nor to specially excepted portions of Virginia and Louisiana, nor to the border states within the Union. Since liberation took place in areas not under Union military control, the proclamation had negligible effect on the immediate freeing of any individuals. Nevertheless, abolitionists hailed the Emancipation Proclamation. Through his action, Lincoln ensured the death of slavery when the war was won. In fact, many slaves already had seized their own freedom in parts of the South occupied by Federal troops.

declare that all persons held as slaves within said designated States and parts of States are, and henceforward shall be, free; and that the Executive Government of the United States, including the military and naval authorities thereof, will recognize and maintain the freedom of said persons.

And I hereby enjoin upon the people so declared to be free to abstain from all violence, unless in necessary self-defense; and I recommend to them that, in all case when allowed, they labor faithfully for reasonable wages.

And I further declare and make known that such persons of suitable condition will be received into the armed service of the United States to garrison forts, positions, stations, and other places, and to man vessels of all sorts in said service.

And upon this act, sincerely believed to be an act of justice, warranted by the Constitution upon military necessity, I invoke the considerate judgment of mankind and the gracious favor of Almighty God.

The Gettysburg Address

On November 19, 1863, the national cemetery at the Gettysburg, Pennsylvania, battlefield was dedicated. The principle oration was delivered by Edward Everett but Lincoln's brief remarks, in the course of which he referred to a "new birth of freedom," is the most memorable of all American addresses.

Lincoln, as president, made few public addresses, the chief examples being his inaugurals, his Gettysburg Address, and his last speech on April 11, 1865. Rather than addresses, Lincoln wrote letters. When answering criticism or appealing to the people, he would prepare a letter which, while addressed to an individual, would be intended for the nation.

Fourscore and seven years ago our fathers brought forth on this continent a new nation, conceived in liberty and dedicated to the proposition that all men are created equal.

Now we are engaged in a great civil war, testing whether that nation or any nation so conceived and so dedicated can long endure. We are met on a great battlefield of that war. We have come to dedicate a portion of that field as a final resting-place for those who here gave their lives that that nation might live. It is altogether fitting and proper that we should do this.

But in a larger sense, we cannot dedicate—we cannot consecrate—we cannot hallow—this ground. The brave men, living and dead, who struggled here have consecrated it far above our poor power to add or detract. The world will little note nor long remember what we say here, but it can never forget what they did here. It is for us the living rather to be dedicated here to the unfinished work which they who fought here have thus far so nobly advanced. It is rather for us to be here dedicated to the great task remaining before us—from these honored dead we take increased devotion to that cause for which they gave the last full measure of devotion—that we here highly resolve that these dead shall not have died in vain—that this nation under God shall have a new birth of freedom—and that government of the people, by the people, for the people shall not perish from the earth.

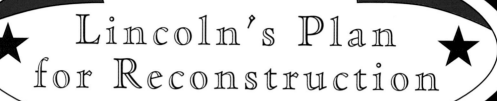

★ Lincoln's Plan for Reconstruction ★

Even though the Civil War would not end until April 1865, in late 1863 Lincoln developed a plan to bring the rebellious states back into the Union. On December 8 he issued this proclamation. It provides a means of pardoning "those who resume their allegiance" to the Union. To those individuals who took an oath of future loyalty, he was prepared to grant amnesty, with some notable exceptions. Those exceptions are specifically listed in the proclamation. He also provided guidelines for the systematic reestablishment of state governments.

WHEREAS, in and by the Constitution of the United States, it is provided that the President "shall have power to grant reprieves and pardons for offences against the United States [and]

Whereas, a rebellion now exists whereby the loyal state governments of several states have for a long time been subverted, and many persons have committed, and are now guilty of, treason against the United States; and

Whereas, with reference to said rebellion and treason, laws have been enacted by congress, declaring forfeitures and confiscation of property and liberation of slaves, all upon terms and conditions therein stated, and also declaring that the President was thereby authorized at any time thereafter, by proclamation, to extend to persons who may have participated in the existing rebellion, in any state or part thereof, pardon and amnesty, with such exceptions and at such times and on such conditions as he may deem expedient for the public welfare; and

Whereas, the congressional declaration for limited and conditional pardon accords with well-established judicial exposition of the pardoning power; and

Whereas, with reference to said rebellion, the President of the United States has issued several proclamations, with provisions in regard to the liberation of slaves; and

Whereas, it is now desired by some persons heretofore engaged in said rebellion to resume their allegiance to the United States, and to reinaugurate loyal state governments within and for their respective states: Therefore—

I, ABRAHAM LINCOLN, President of the United States, do proclaim, declare, and make known to all persons who have, directly or by implication, participated in the existing rebellion, except as hereinafter excepted, that a full pardon is hereby granted to them and each of them, with restoration of all rights of property, except as to slaves, and in property cases where rights of third parties shall have intervened, and upon the condition that every such person shall take and subscribe an oath, and thence-forward keep and maintain said oath inviolate; and which oath shall be registered for permanent preservation, and shall be of the tenor and effect following, to wit:

> "I,   , do solemnly swear, in presence of Almighty God, that I will henceforth faithfully support, protect, and defend the Constitution of the United States and the Union of the States thereunder; and that I will, in like manner, abide by and faithfully support all acts of congress passed during the existing rebellion with reference to slaves, so long and so far as not repealed, modified, or held void by congress, or by decision of the supreme court; and that I will, in like manner, abide by and faithfully support all proclamations of the President made during the existing rebellion having reference to slaves, so long and so far as not modified or declared void by decision of the supreme court. So help me God."

The persons excepted from the benefits of the foregoing provisions are all who are, or shall have been, civil or diplomatic officers or agents of the so-called Confederate government; all who have left judicial stations under the United States to aid the rebellion; all who are, or shall have been, military or naval officers of said so-called Confederate government above the rank of colonel in the army or of lieutenant in the navy; all who left seats in the United States congress to aid the rebellion; all who resigned commissions in the army or navy of the United States and afterwards aided the rebellion; and all who have engaged in any way in treating colored persons, or white persons in charge of such, otherwise than lawfully as prisoners of war, and which persons may have been found in the United States service as soldiers, seamen, or in any other capacity.

And I do further proclaim, declare, and make known that whenever, in any of the States of Arkansas, Texas, Louisiana, Mississippi, Tennessee, Alabama, Georgia, Florida, South Carolina, and North Carolina, a number of persons,

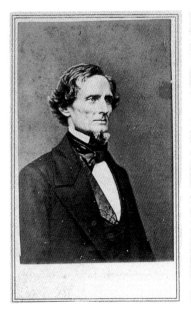 

Jefferson Davis and Alexander Stephens, cartes de visite. Stephens was vice president of the Confederacy.

General Robert E. Lee surrendered at Appomattox Courthouse, a village some ninety-five miles west of Richmond, on April 9, 1865. This was the military conclusion to the Civil War (although some Confederate military units would not surrender for another two months). However, Jefferson Davis and his cabinet remained at large, moving southward as fast as the dilapidated railroad system could carry them. At every stop, Davis pleaded with well-wishers to fight on "operating in the interior where the enemy's extended lines of communication would render our triumph certain." Davis spoke of moving the Confederate government to the trans-Mississippi states and continuing the war. He promised that Richmond would soon be retaken. On April 24, at Charlotte, North Carolina, Davis finally admitted that the Confederacy had been defeated. He continued southward hoping to escape out of the country. At Irwinville, Georgia, he was captured by Federal cavalry on May 10. Davis spent two years in prison, at times in irons. He was released on bond in 1867. Horace Greeley, once a bitter enemy of everything Southern, was among his bondsmen.

Alexander Stephens was arrested at his Georgia home on May 11, 1865, and moved to a prison in Boston harbor. Released on parole on October 12, he was warmly greeted by throngs at New York, Washington, and Atlanta as he traveled home. At his Georgia plantation, he dwelt much as before, with former slaves continuing to serve him.

not less than one tenth in number of the votes cast in such state at the presidential election of the year of our Lord one thousand eight hundred and sixty, each having taken the oath aforesaid, and not having since violated it, and being a qualified voter by the election law of the state existing immediately before the so-called act of secession, and excluding all others, shall reëstablish a state government which shall be republican, and in nowise contravening said oath, such shall be recognized as the true government of the state, and the state shall receive thereunder the benefits of the constitutional provision which declares that "the United States shall guaranty to every state in this Union a republican form of government, and shall protect each of them against invasion; and on application of the legislature, or the executive, (when the legislature cannot be convened,) against domestic violence."

And I do further proclaim, declare, and make known that any provision which may be adopted by such state government in relation to the freed people of such state, which shall recognize and declare their permanent freedom, provide for their education, and which may yet be consistent as a temporary arrangement with their present condition as a laboring, landless, and homeless class, will not be objected to by the National Executive.

And it is suggested as not improper that, in constructing a loyal state government in any state, the name of the state, the boundary, the subdivisions, the constitution, and the general code of laws, as before the rebellion, be maintained, subject only to the modifications made necessary by the conditions hereinbefore stated, and such others, if any, not contravening said conditions, and which may be deemed expedient by those framing the new state government.

To avoid misunderstanding, it may be proper to say that this proclamation, so far as it relates to state governments, has no reference to states wherein loyal state governments have all the while been maintained. And, for the same reason, it may be proper to further say, that whether members sent to congress from any state shall be admitted to seats constitutionally rests exclusively with the respective houses, and not to any extent with the Executive. And still further, that this proclamation is intended to present the people of the states wherein the national authority has been suspended, and loyal state governments have been subverted, a mode in and by which the national authority and loyal state governments may be reëstablished within said states, or in any of them; and while the mode presented is the best the Executive can suggest, with his present impressions, it must not be understood that no other possible mode would be acceptable.

Lincoln's Veto of the Wade-Davis Bill

The Radical Republicans were a faction within the Republican Party that favored emancipation as a war goal and equality for the freedmen in the reconstructed South. They did not share Lincoln's belief that white Southerners could be trusted with deciding the future of the newly freed black people. In July 1864, a major breach developed between Lincoln and the radicals over the manner and method of reconstructing the union after the war ended. The President used the pocket veto to kill the Wade-Davis bill, the radical Republican plan which enabled only those Southerners who had *always* been loyal to the Union and had not "voluntarily borne arms against the United States" to participate in the reconstruction process. Lincoln issued this statement explaining his reasons for the veto.

WHEREAS, at the late Session, Congress passed a Bill, "To guarantee to certain States, whose governments have been usurped or overthrown, a republican form of Government," a copy of which is hereunto annexed:

And whereas, the said Bill was presented to the President of the United States, for his approval, less than one hour before the *sine die* adjournment of said Session, and was not signed by him:

And whereas, the said Bill contains, among other things, a plan for restoring the States in rebellion to their proper practical relation in the Union [. . .]

Now, therefore, I, Abraham Lincoln, President of the United States, do proclaim, declare, and make known, that, while I am, (as I was in December last, when by proclamation I propounded a plan for restoration) unprepared, by a formal approval of this Bill, to be inflexibly committed to any single plan of restoration; and, while I am also unprepared to declare, that the free-state constitutions and governments, already adopted and installed in Arkansas and Louisiana, shall be set aside and held for nought, thereby repelling and discouraging the loyal citizens who have set up the same, as to further effort; or to declare a constitutional competency in Congress to abolish slavery in States, but am at the same time sincerely hoping and expecting that a constitutional amendment, abolishing slavery throughout the nation, may be adopted, nevertheless, I am fully satisfied with the system for restoration contained in the Bill, as one very proper plan for the loyal people of any State choosing to adopt it; and that I am, and at all times shall be, prepared to give the Executive aid and assistance to any such people, so soon as the military resistance to the United States shall have been suppressed in any such State, and the people thereof shall have sufficiently returned to their obedience to the Constitution and the laws of the United States,-in which cases, military Governors will be appointed, with directions to proceed according to the Bill.

The Wade-Davis Manifesto

Benjamin Wade, chairman of the Senate committee on Territories, and Henry Winter Davis, chairman of a special House reconstruction committee, were Radical Republicans. Wade and Davis decided to issue their own response to Lincoln's veto. As they drafted it, their bitterness toward Lincoln carried them into rhetorical excess. "He must understand," they declared, "that our support is of a cause and not of a man." They accused Lincoln of assuming "dictatorial power" instead of confining himself to obeying and executing the law. This "manifesto" is an astonishing attack on a president by leaders of his own party and demonstrates a rift among Republicans over what should be done with the South after the war ended.

We have read without surprise, but not without indignation, the Proclamation of the President of the 8th of July.

The President, by preventing this bill from becoming a law, holds the electoral votes of the Rebel States at the dictation of his personal ambition.

If those votes turn the balance in his favor, is it to be supposed that his competitor, defeated by such means will acquiesce?

If the Rebel majority assert their supremacy in those States, and send votes which elect an enemy of the Government, will we not repel his claims?

And is not that civil war for the Presidency, inaugurated by the votes of Rebel States?

Seriously impressed with these dangers, Congress, "*the proper constitutional authority*," formally declared that there are no State Governments in the Rebel States, and provided for their erection at a proper time; and both the Senate and the House of Representatives rejected the Senators and Representatives chosen under the authority of what the President calls the Free Constitution and Government of Arkansas.

The President's proclamation "*holds for naught*" this judgment, and discards the authority of the Supreme Court, and strides headlong toward the anarchy his Proclamation of the 8th of December inaugurated.

If electors for President be allowed to be chosen in either of those States, a sinister light will be cast on the motives which induced the President to "*hold for naught*" the will of Congress rather than his Government in Louisiana and Arkansas.

That judgment of Congress which the President defies was the exercise of an authority exclusively vested in Congress by the Constitution to determine what is the established Government in a State, and in its own nature and by the highest judicial authority binding on all other departments of the Government.

A more studied outrage on the legislative authority of the people has never been perpetrated. Congress passed a bill; the President refused to approve it, and then by proclamation puts as much of it in force as he sees fit, and proposes to execute those parts by officers unknown to the laws of the United States and not subject to the confirmation of the Senate!

The bill directed the appointment of Provisional Governors by and with the advice and consent of the Senate.

The President, after defeating the law, proposes to appoint without law, and without the advice and consent of the Senate, *Military* Governors for the Rebel States!

He has already exercised this dictatorial usurpation in Louisiana, and he defeated the bill to prevent its limitation.

The President has greatly presumed on the forbearance which the supporters of his Administration have so long practiced, in view of the arduous conflict in which we are engaged, and the reckless ferocity of our political opponents.

But he must understand that our support is of a cause and not of a man; that the authority of Congress is paramount and must be respected; that the whole body of the Union men of Congress will not submit to be impeached by him of rash and unconstitutional legislation; and if he wishes our support, he must confine himself to his executive duties—to obey and execute, not make the laws—to suppress by arms armed Rebellion, and leave political reorganization to Congress.

(Opposite) Envelopes styled after the Confederate flag. (Right) Jefferson Davis sheet music.

Confederate veterans returned to a ruined land. In addition to physical devastation, the South had suffered a severe economic disruption. Confederate money was worthless. Southern banks were ruined. And, for Southern planters, the severest economic blow was the freeing of their slaves. The disorganization of agriculture was so great that in 1866, the first year after the war had ended, cotton production was less than half of what it had been in 1860.

In 1865, Lincoln believed that all black people should be free. Beyond that, he thought Southerners should work out the details of the transition from bondage to freedom. Lincoln's lenient policy toward Southern whites was opposed by the Radical Republicans, who had a majority in Congress. They argued that the states which had seceded from the Union were no longer states but conquered territories. They believed it was for Congress, rather than the president, to determine reconstruction policy. Had Lincoln lived, Congress might well have prevented him from implementing a peace based on "malice toward none" and "charity for all."

If the supporters of the Government fail to insist on this, they become responsible for the usurpations which they fail to rebuke, and are justly liable to the indignation of the people whose rights and security, committed to their keeping, they sacrifice.

Let them consider the remedy for these usurpations, and, having found it, fearlessly execute it.

Lincoln's Second Inaugural Address

Lincoln delivered his short but brilliant Second Inaugural Address—just a little under 700 words—on March 4, 1865. For four years, the crusade to save the Union had raged and now it neared a successful conclusion. Four years of death and destruction had created an atmosphere of vindictiveness. But Lincoln's memorable address stands above the hate that preceded, accompanied, and followed this horrible war. In twenty-six sentences he soared above momentary passions to capture something of the larger tragedy involved. There was one new and striking feature in the simple inaugural ceremony—the presence of a battalion of African-American troops in the escort party.

At this second appearing to take the oath of the Presidential office there is less occasion for an extended address than there was at the first. Then a statement somewhat in detail of a course to be pursued seemed fitting and proper. Now, at the expiration of four years, during which public declarations have been constantly called forth on every point and phase of the great contest which still absorbs the attention and engrosses the energies of the nation, little that is new could be presented. The progress of our arms, upon which all else chiefly depends, is as well known to the public as to myself, and it is, I trust, reasonably satisfactory and encouraging to all. With high hope for the future, no prediction in regard to it is ventured.

On the occasion corresponding to this four years ago all thoughts were anxiously directed to an impending civil war. All dreaded it, all sought to avert it. While the inaugural address was being delivered from this place, devoted altogether to saving the Union without war, urgent agents were in the city seeking to destroy it without war—seeking to dissolve the Union and divide effects by negotiation. Both parties deprecated war, but one of them would make war rather than let the nation survive, and the other would accept war rather than let it perish, and the war came.

One-eighth of the whole population were colored slaves, not distributed generally over the Union, but localized in the southern part of it. These slaves constituted a peculiar and powerful interest. All knew that this interest was somehow the cause of the war. To strengthen, perpetuate, and extend this interest was the object for which the insurgents would rend the Union even by war, while the Government claimed no right to do more than to restrict the territorial enlargement of it. Neither party expected for the war the magnitude or the duration which it has already attained. Neither anticipated that the cause of the conflict might cease with or even before the conflict itself should cease. Each looked for

Woven silk ribbon imported from Switzerland for Lincoln's 1861 inauguration. The image was taken from a Currier & Ives print after a Brady photo.

an easier triumph, and a result less fundamental and astounding. Both read the same Bible and pray to the same God, and each invokes His aid against the other. It may seem strange that any men should dare to ask a just God's assistance in wringing their bread from the sweat of other men's faces, but let us judge not, that we be not judged. The prayers of both could not be answered. That of neither has been answered fully. The Almighty has His own purposes. "Woe unto the world because of offenses; for it must needs be that offenses come, but woe to that man by whom the offense cometh." If we shall suppose that American slavery is one of those offenses which, in the providence of God, must needs come, but which, having continued through His appointed time, He now wills to remove, and that He gives to both North and South this terrible war as the woe due to those by whom the offense came, shall we discern therein any departure from those divine attributes which the believers in a living God always ascribe to Him? Fondly do we hope, fervently do we pray, that this mighty scourge of war may speedily pass away. Yet, if God wills that it continue until all the wealth piled by the bondsman's two hundred and fifty years of unrequited toil shall be sunk, and until every drop of blood drawn with the lash shall be paid by another drawn with the sword, as was said three thousand years ago, so still it must be said "the judgments of the Lord are true and righteous altogether."

With malice toward none, with charity for all, with firmness in the right as God gives us to see the right, let us strive on to finish the work we are in, to bind up the nation's wounds, to care for him who shall have borne the battle and for his widow and his orphan, to do all which may achieve and cherish a just and lasting peace among ourselves and with all nations.

GENERAL REFERENCE

Israel, Fred L. *Student's Atlas of American Presidential Elections, 1789–1996*. Washington, D.C.: Congressional Quarterly Books, 1998.

Levy, Peter B., editor. *100 Key Documents in American History*. Westport, Conn.: Praeger, 1999.

Mieczkowski, Yarek. *The Routledge Historical Atlas of Presidential Elections*. New York: Routledge, 2001.

Polsby, Nelson W., and Aaron Wildavsky. *Presidential Elections: Strategies and Structures of American Politics*. 10th edition. New York: Chatham House, 2000.

Watts, J. F., and Fred L. Israel, editors. *Presidential Documents*. New York: Routledge, 2000.

Widmer, Ted. *The New York Times Campaigns: A Century of Presidential Races*. New York: DK Publishing, 2000.

POLITICAL AMERICANA REFERENCE

Cunningham, Noble E. Jr. *Popular Images of the Presidency: From Washington to Lincoln*. Columbia: University of Missouri Press, 1991.

Melder, Keith. *Hail to the Candidate: Presidential Campaigns from Banners to Broadcasts*. Washington, D.C.: Smithsonian Institution Press, 1992.

Schlesinger, Arthur M. jr., Fred L. Israel, and David J. Frent. *Running for President: The Candidates and their Images*. 2 vols. New York: Simon and Schuster, 1994.

Warda, Mark. *100 Years of Political Campaign Collectibles*. Clearwater, Fla.: Galt Press, 1996.

THE ELECTION OF 1860
and the Administration of Abraham Lincoln

Burchard, Peter. *Lincoln & Slavery*. New York: Atheneum Press, 1999.

Dilorenzo, Thomas J. *The Real Lincoln: A New Look at Abraham Lincoln, his Agenda, and an Unnecessary War*. Rocklin, Calif.: Prima Publishing, 2002.

Freedman, Russell. *Lincoln: A Photobiography*. Boston: Houghton Mifflin, 1987.

Gienapp, William E. *Abraham Lincoln and Civil War America*. New York: Oxford University Press, 2002.

Holzer, Harold. *Abraham Lincoln the Writer: A Treasury of His Great Speeches and Letters*. Honesdale, Pa.: Boyds Mill Press, 2000.

Jones, Lynda. *Abe Lincoln*. New York: Scholastic Trade, 2000.

Kigel, Richard. *The Frontier Years of Abraham Lincoln*. New York: Walker and Company, 1986.

Miller, William Lee. *Lincoln's Virtues: An Ethical Biography*. New York: Knopf, 2002.

Steers, Edward J. *Blood on the Moon: The Assassination of Abraham Lincoln*. Lexington: University Press of Kentucky, 2001.

White, Ronald C. Jr., *Lincoln's Greatest Speech: The Second Inaugural*. New York: Simon and Schuster, 2002.

Wills, Gary. *Lincoln at Gettysburg: The Words that Remade America*. New York: Simon and Schuster, 1992.

INDEX

A

Alabama, 33, 79
Arkansas, 113, 115
Articles of Association (1774), 71
    See also Union, Federal
Articles of Confederation (1778), 71
    See also Union, Federal
Atlanta, Georgia, 40, *109*

B

Bell, John, 17, 18, 19, 21, *23*, 24, *29*, 30, 31, 35, 37, 58
    electoral votes for, *41*
Belmont, Augustus, 19
Booth, John Wilkes, 40
Boteler, Alexander, 21
Brady, Matthew, *18*, *21*, *29*, *39*, *91*, *120*
Breckinridge, John C., 17, 18, 19, 21, 24, 25, *29*, 32, 33, 35, 37, 54
    electoral votes for, *41*
Buchanan, James, 25, 28, 45

C

campaigning, 8–14
    and the 1860 election, 17–37
    cartoons, 29–30, 37
    literature, 19, 21, 23, 24
    mass meetings, 25–26
    songs, 28–29
    speaking tours, 32–33
cartoons, campaign, 29–30
Central Pacific Railroad Company, 94, 97

    See also railroad, transcontinental
Charleston, South Carolina, 78
Charlotte, North Carolina, *109*
Chicago, Illinois, 24, 25
Chicago Tribune, 23, 42, *52*
Cincinnati, Ohio, 55, 56
Civil War, *109*
    casualties, *83*
    origins, 37, 40, 77, 78–85
    and Reconstruction, 106–108, 110–111, 113
Cleveland, Grover, *52*
Cleveland, John F., 21
Codding, Ichabod, 21, 23
Compromise of 1850, 60
    See also slavery
Confederate States of America, 40, *63*, 80, *96*, *109*
Congress, message to (1861), 78–87
Constitution, United States, 44, 49, 53, 55–56, 67, 71, 77, 99
    amendments to, 75–76
    and the Constitutional Union party, 58–59
    and the fugitive slave law, 68–69, 74–75
    and political parties, 6–8
    and Reconstruction, 107
    and secession, 82–84
    and slavery, 46, 49, 60–62, 64–65, 73
Constitutional Union party, 17, *18*, 31–32, *41*
    platform (1860), 58–59
    See also parties, political
constitutions, state, 43, 56, 113

Numbers in **bold italics** refer to captions.

Crittenden, John J., 60–62, 64–65
Crittenden Compromise, 60–62, 64–65
    See also slavery
Cuba, 55, 57
Currier and Ives, 30, *120*

D
Davis, Henry Winter, 114
Davis, Jefferson, *63*, *86*, *96*, *109*, *116*, *117*
Declaration of Independence (1776), 48, 49, 71
Delaware, 100
Democratic party, 30, 49
    division in, 17, 54
    See also Northern Democrats; parties,
        political; Southern Democrats
Douglas, Stephen A., 10–11, 42, 45–46
    electoral votes for, *41*
    memorabilia, *19*, *21*, *29*, *30*, *31*, *32*
    as presidential candidate, 17–18, 19, 23, 25,
        31–33, 35, 37, 54
Douglas Democrats. See Northern Democrats
Dred Scott decision, 43, 44–46
    See also slavery

E
election, presidential
    and campaigning, 8–14, 17–37
    electoral votes (1860), 37, *41*
    importance of, in 1860, 17, *70*
    popular interest in, 18, 37
    process of, 6, 15
electoral college, 37, *41*, 115
Emancipation Proclamation, 40, 100–103
Everett, Edward, *18*, *23*, 58, 104

F
Federal Union. See Union, Federal
ferrotypes. See memorabilia, political
Florida, 79, 82
Fogg, George G., 19
Forsythe, John, 24
Fort Sumter, 40, 78, 79–82
Frank Leslie's Illustrated Newspaper, *70*
fugitive slave law, 55–56, 57, 64–65, 68, 74–75
    See also slavery

G
Gadsden Purchase, *96*
Georgia, 19, 33, *63*, 79
Gettysburg Address, 104–105
Gettysburg, Pennsylvania, 40, 104–105
government, Federal, 49, 76, 82
Grant, Ulysses S., 40
Greeley, Horace, 11, 21, 30, 98–99, *109*

H
Hamlin, Hannibal, 38, *86*
Hanks, John, 27–28
Harper's Weekly, 34
Hartford, Connecticut, 34–35
Homestead Act (1862), 48, 53, 88–93
"House Divided" speech (1858), 42–47
    See also speeches
House of Representatives, 18, 51, 61, 64, 89,
    115
Howells, William Dean, 23

I
Illinois, 17, 21, *22*, 25, 28, 54, 66
immigrants, 23
immigration policy, 48, 53
inaugural address
    Abraham Lincoln's first, 66–69, 71–77
    Abraham Lincoln's second, 118–121
Indiana, 33
Irwinville, Georgia, *109*

J
Jefferson, Thomas, 7, 12, 85
Johnson, Andrew, 10–11, 38

K
Kansas-Nebraska Act (1854), 60
    See also slavery
Kansas (territory), 45–46, 49, 51
Kentucky, 38, *41*, 60
King, Preston, 19

L
Lane, Joseph, *19*
Lee, Robert E., 40, *109*

Lincoln, Abraham, 10, 11, 15, 33, 107–108
   and "Abe" nickname, 28
   and the Civil War, 78–87
   electoral votes for (1860), 37, *41*
   Emancipation Proclamation of, 40, 100–103
   facts at a glance, 38–41
   and the Gettysburg Address, 104–105
   and Horace Greeley, 98–99
   and the "House Divided" speech (1858),
      42–47
   inaugural addresses of, 66–69, 71–77,
      118–121
   memorabilia, *18*, *26*, *27*, *31*, *32*, *35*, *39*, *51*,
      91, *92*, *120*
   and the Pacific Railway Act, 94–97
   political positions of, 39
   portrait of, *70*, *83*, *86*, *102*
   and preservation of the Union, 66, 98–99
   as presidential candidate, 17–18, 19, 21, *22,*
      23, 26–29, 30, 33–34, 37
   Reconstruction plan of, 106–108, 110–111,
      113, *117*
   and the Wade-Davis bill, 112–113, 114–117
Lincoln, Mary Todd (Mrs. Abraham Lincoln), 38,
   102
Lincoln-Douglas debates (1858), 21
literature, campaign, 19, 21, 23, 24
Louisiana, 19, 79, 103, 113, 115, 116

M

Marcy, William, *96*
Maryland, 62
McCormick, Cyrus, 24
memorabilia, political, *18*, *19*, *20*, *24*, *25*, *29*,
   30–31, *52*, *86*, *116*, *117*
   and Abraham Lincoln, *18*, *26*, *27*, *31*, *32*,
      35, *39*, *51*, *91*, *92*, *120*
   and Stephen A. Douglas, *19*, *21*, *29*, *30*,
      31, *32*
Mexico, 48, *96*
Mississippi, *63*, 79, 93
Missouri, 100
Missouri Compromise (1820), 60
   See also slavery
Montgomery, Alabama, *63*
Morgan, Edwin D., 19

N

naturalization. See immigration policy
Nebraska doctrine, 43, 44–46
   See also slavery
Nebraska (territory), 51
New Jersey, 31, 48
New Orleans, Louisiana, 32
New York, 19, 24, 32–33, *109*
New York City, 32–33, *34*, *36*, 37, *91*
New York Tribune, 23, 30, 98–99
newspapers. See press
Northern Democrats, 17, 18, 19
   platform (1860), 54–56
   See also Democratic party

O

Oglesby, Richard, 28
Ohio, 33
Oregon, 21

P

Pacific Railway Act, 94–97
   See also railroad, transcontinental
parties, political
   and campaigning, 11–13, 17
   platforms of, 9, 10, 48–52, 53, 54–59
Pennsylvania, 31, 33, 48
photographs. See memorabilia, political
Pierce, Franklin, *96*
platforms, political party, 9, 10, 17
   Constitutional Union (1860), 58–59
   Democratic (1860), 54–57
   Republican (1860), 48–51, 53
Political Textbook for 1860, 21
popular sovereignty, 17, 32, 51, 54
   See also Douglas, Stephen A.; Northern
      Democrats
President, United States
   role of, 6–7, 13–14, 76, 85–87, 107
press (in the 1860 election), 23–24, 32–33

R

The Rail Splitter, 24
railroad, transcontinental, 48, 53, 55, 57, 94–97
Reconstruction, 106–108, 110–111, 113, *117*
Register (Mobile), 24

Republican party, 17, 18, 19, **22**, 31, 32–33, 37, 47, **52**, **70**
  campaign literature of, 21, 23, 24, 29–30
  and campaign pageantry, 25–29
  platform (1860), 48–51, 53
  Radical Republicans, 112, 114, **117**
  and slavery, 45–46
  Wide-Awake society, **33**, 34–35, 37
  See also parties, political
Richmond, Virginia, **109**

S

Schurz, Carl, 23
Scripps, John Locke, 23
secession, 33, 37, 40, 60–61, **63**, 73–74, 80
  and the Constitution, 82–84, 93
Senate, 42, 61, 64, 89, 115–116
Sheehan, James W., 23
slave trade, 51, 65, 75
  See also slavery
slavery, 58, 74–75, 93, **117**
  and Abraham Lincoln, 23, 43–47, 67, 98–99, 119–120
  compromises on, 60–62, 64–65
  and the Democratic Party split, 17, 54
  and the Emancipation Proclamation, 40, 100–103
  in the territories, 17, 44–47, 48, 49–51, 55–57, 62, 73
songs, campaign, 28–29
South Carolina, 40, 60, 78, 79, 84, 93
Southern Democrats, 17, **52**
  platform (1860), 54, 56–57
  See also Democratic party
Spain, 55, 57
speeches, 11, 14, 104
  and the 1860 campaign, 18–19, 26, 32–33, 37
  first inaugural address (Abraham Lincoln), 66–69, 71–77
  Gettsyburg Address, 104–105
  "House Divided" (1858), 42–47
  message to Congress (1861), 78–87
  second inaugural address (Abraham Lincoln), 118–121
states' rights, 48, 49–50, 56, 67–68, 76, 82, 84
Stephens, Alexander H., 19, **63**, **86**, **109**

Stevens, Isaac, 19, 21
Supreme Court, United States, 45, 55–56, 64, 74

T

tariffs, 31, 48, 53
Taylor, Moses, 19
Tennessee, 17, 33, **41**, 58, 84, 103
territories, 56, 114
  slavery in, 17, 44–47, 48, 49–51, 55–56, 62, 73
Texas, 83
Thirteenth Amendment, 100
Times (Chicago), 23, 24
Tribune (Chicago), 23, 42, 52
Tribune (New York), 23, 30, 98–99

U

Union, Federal, 43, 49, 56, 58–59
  and Abraham Lincoln, 66, 69, 71–73, 75, 78, 98–99, 118
  and the Civil War, 80–82, 84–85
  and Reconstruction, 106–108, 110–111, 113, **117**
  and slavery compromises, 60–62, 64–65
Union Pacific Railroad Company, 94, 95, 97
  See also railroad, transcontinental

V

Vermont, 32
Virginia, 21, **41**, 62, 84, 103

W

Wade, Benjamin, 114
Wade-Davis bill, 112–113
Wade-Davis manifesto, 114–117
Washington, D.C., 19, 21, 25, 38, 62, 66, **109**
Washington, George, 7, 14, 85
West, settlement of, 90, **92**
Whig party, 9, 10, 17, 58
  See also Constitutional Union party; parties, political
Wide-Awake society, **33**, 34–35, 37
Wilmot Proviso, 48

The EDITORS

ARTHUR M. SCHLESINGER JR. holds the Albert Schweitzer Chair in the Humanities at the Graduate Center of the City University of New York. He is the author of more than a dozen books, including *The Age of Jackson*; *The Vital Center*; *The Age of Roosevelt* (3 vols.); *A Thousand Days: John F. Kennedy in the White House*; *Robert Kennedy and His Times*; *The Cycles of American History*; and *The Imperial Presidency*. Professor Schlesinger served as Special Assistant to President Kennedy (1961–63). His numerous awards include: the Pulitzer Prize for History; the Pulitzer Prize for Biography; two National Book Awards; The Bancroft Prize; and the American Academy of Arts and Letters Gold Medal for History.

FRED L. ISRAEL is the senior professor of American history at the City College of New York. He is the author of *Nevada's Key Pittman* and has edited *The War Diary of Breckinridge Long* and *Major Peace Treaties of Modern History, 1648–1975* (5 vols.) He holds the Scribe's Award from the American Bar Association for his joint editorship of the *Justices of the United States Supreme Court* (4 vols.). For more than 25 years Professor Israel has compiled and edited the Gallup Poll into annual reference volumes.

DAVID J. FRENT is the president of Political Americana Auctions, Oakhurst, NJ. With his wife, Janice, he has assembled the nation's foremost private collection of political campaign memorabilia. Mr. Frent has designed exhibits for corporations, the Smithsonian Institution, and the United States Information Agency. A member of the board of directors of the American Political Items Collectors since 1972, he was elected to its Hall of Fame for his "outstanding contribution to preserving and studying our political heritage."